DHARMA OCEAN SERIES

In a meeting with Samuel Bercholz, the president of
Shambhala Publications, Ven. Chögyam Trungpa ex-
pressed his interest in publishing a series of 108
volumes, to be called the Dharma Ocean Series.
"Dharma Ocean" is the translation of Chögyam
Trungpa's Tibetan teaching name, Chökyi Gyatso.
The Dharma Ocean Series consists primarily of edited
transcripts of lectures and seminars given by Chögyam
Trungpa during his seventeen years of teaching in
North America. The goal of the series is to allow
readers to encounter this rich array of teachings simply and directly rather than in an overly systematized
or condensed form. At its completion, it will serve as
the literary archive of the major works of this
renowned Tibetan Buddhist teacher.

Series Editor: Judith L. Lief

DHARMA OCEAN SERIES

Illusion's Game

THE LIFE AND TEACHING OF NAROPA

Chögyam Trungpa

Edited by Sherab Chödzin

Shambhala · Boston & London · 1994

SHAMBHALA PUBLICATIONS, INC.
Horticultural Hall
300 Massachusetts Avenue
Boston, Massachusetts 02115
www.shambhala.com

Printed in the United States of America

Distributed in the United States by Random House, Inc.,
and in Canada by Random House of Canada Ltd

LIBRARY OF CONGRESS CATALOGING-IN-PUBLICATION DATA

Trungpa, Chögyam, 1939–
    Illusion's game: the life and teaching of Naropa / Chögyam Trungpa: edited by Sherab Chödzin.—1st ed.
        p.   cm.—(Dharma ocean series)
    Includes index.
    ISBN 0-87773-857-2
    1. Naḍapāda.   2. Yoga (Tantric Buddhism)   I. Chödzin, Sherab
    II. Series: Trungpa, Chögyam, 1939–   Dharma ocean series.
BQ7950.N347T78   1994   93-39383
294.3'925'092—dc20   CIP

BVG 01

Contents

Editor's Foreword   vii

PART ONE
"LIFE OF NAROPA" SEMINAR I
New York, 1972
1   Naropa and Us   3
2   Genuine Madness and Pop Art   8
3   An Operation without Anesthetics   32
4   Something Very Tickling   50

PART TWO
"LIFE OF NAROPA" SEMINAR II
Karmê-Chöling, 1973
1   Pain and Hopelessness   55
2   Giving Birth to Intellect   69
3   Choiceless Awareness   87
4   Beyond Shunyata   100
5   Mahamudra   116
6   The Levels of Mahamudra   131

vi • CONTENTS

Notes 151
Glossary 153
Transliteration of Tibetan Terms 162
About the Author 163
Meditation Center Information 168
Index 171

Editor's Foreword

THIS BOOK IS composed of two seminars by the Vidyadhara, the Venerable Chögyam Trungpa, Rinpoche, on the life and teachings of Naropa. Naropa, an Indian of the eleventh century, was one of the Vidyadhara's own spiritual forefathers and a seminal figure for the vajrayana buddhism of Tibet. The Vidyadhara gave a number of seminars on Naropa, each with its own flavor and emphasis. The editor has had to make a more or less arbitrary selection from them for this volume (New York, January 1972, four talks; Tail of the Tiger, Vermont, 1973, six talks). Future volumes, we hope, will complete the availability to the public of the Vidyadhara's teaching on the very profound subject matter surrounding the life of Naropa.

"Great Vajradhara, Telo, Naro, Marpa, Mila; lord of dharma, Gampopa. . . ." So begins the supplication to the lineage of enlightened teachers of the Kagyu, one of the four main orders of Buddhism in Tibet. Vajradhara is the *dharmakaya* buddha, the ultimate repository of awakened mind. Telo is Tilopa, a great Indian *siddha*, Naropa's guru, the first human in the lineage. Naro is Naropa, who became the guru of Marpa, the first Tibetan in the lineage. Marpa's disciple was Mila, the renowned Tibetan yogi usually known as Milarepa (Mila the cotton clad). Milarepa's leading disciple, Gampopa, founded the monastic order of the Kagyu, the various branches of which have been headed by Gampopa's successors for the last nine hundred years.

In the vajrayana buddhism of Tibet, the central event, which remains timelessly new through the generations, is the transmission of the awakened state of mind from guru to disciple through a meeting of minds. As the awakened state itself is independent of word, concept, or thought, the transmission of it is beyond process. Nevertheless it happens in people's lives, and an extraordinarily demanding process of preparation seems to be needed for students to reach the spiritual nakedness that enables them to open directly to the guru's mind. This process, as we see from Naropa's story, is one that requires of the student an extreme level of self-surrender and in which the teacher sometimes resorts to extremely brutal means to break him and strip him down. Doubtless to the workaday world, such a process, with its outrageous suffering, may seem insane. Yet, seen with the greater vision of enlightenment—here spoken of in terms of *mahamudra,* the "great seal"—this process is the utmost expression of compassion and sanity. The tale of how Naropa came into direct communication with Tilopa and received from him the transmission of awakened mind became a paradigm for the later tradition of vajrayana buddhism in Tibet, which arose out of their relationship.

Naropa's story makes it possible to delineate in very concrete terms the various levels of spiritual development that lead up to the possibility of meeting the guru's mind. This is the main thrust of the Vidyadhara's presentation to Western students—making them see themselves and their potentialities in Naropa and his journey. In this manner he opens to them the path of devotion and surrender to the guru as the embodiment and spokesman of reality. The Vidyadhara deals only briefly here with the formal mahamudra teachings and other tantric teachings associated with Naropa's name, notably, the six dharmas of Naropa (Tib. naro chödruk), or six Naropa yogas, as they are sometimes called. But in his concise descriptions, particularly in the later part of the book, he catches each one by its experiential essence, conveying in a few simple words an insight that students might well seek in vain elsewhere through hundreds of pages of text or many hours of oral teaching.

The students to whom the Vidyadhara gave these talks were asked to read *The Life and Teaching of Naropa,* the twelfth-century biography translated from Tibetan by the eminent scholar Herbert V. Guenther (Boston: Shambhala Publications, 1986). Reading this book might be a help for readers of the present volume. Nevertheless, the summary of it that follows and the citations and references in the text convey the essentials. Moreover, occasional references and descriptions by the Vidyadhara reveal that he was sometimes referring in his own mind to at least one other version of Naropa's life story.

Naropa lived in northern India in the eleventh century. He was the only son of a royal family. From an early age, he devoted himself single-mindedly to spiritual matters. His mind was filled with compassion for beings, and his primary interest was the study and practice of the buddhadharma. In his youth, in view of his parents' strong desire for the continuity of their royal line, Naropa consented to marry. However, after eight years he was once more overcome by his desire to devote himself exclusively to the dharma. His wife, Niguma, agreed to a divorce and became his disciple (and later a great teacher). Naropa entered the great Buddhist monastic university of Nalanda. There he greatly developed his intellectual powers and became extremely learned. So great were his intellectual powers and erudition that he was elevated to the abbacy of Nalanda. He became renowned as the premier teacher of Buddhism of his time.

At this point in his life (at around the age of forty), the event occurred that was to make Naropa of interest to the tantric tradition. One day, as he was reading with his back to the sun (a symbolic description of his spiritual relationship to reality at that time), he had a vision of a very ugly woman, who told him he understood only the words in his book, not their real meaning. She also revealed that the only way to discover the real meaning was to seek a guru, her brother Tilopa (see pages 5–6 for a quotation of this passage). Over the sustained and impassioned objections of the masters and students of Nalanda, who begged Naropa not to leave and deprive them of their guiding light, Naropa departed from the great university and began his lonely journey in search of Tilopa.

This journey turned out to be arduous and daunting in the extreme. Naropa encountered, instead of Tilopa himself, eleven hideous visions (see pages 8–16 for a quotation describing this part of the story). Naropa was about to kill himself when Tilopa finally appeared and accepted him as his student. Tilopa showed Naropa a series of symbols, which Naropa understood. Tilopa then sat motionless for a year. At the end of a year, Tilopa made a slight movement, which provided a pretext for Naropa to prostrate and ask for teaching. Tilopa required him to leap from the roof of a tall temple building. Naropa's body was crushed. He suffered immense pain. Tilopa healed him with a touch of his hand, then gave him instruction.

This pattern was repeated eleven more times. Eleven more times Tilopa remained either motionless or aloof for a year; then Naropa prostrated and asked for teaching. Tilopa caused him to throw himself into a fire, where he was thoroughly burned, be beaten nearly to death, have his blood sucked out by leeches, be pricked with flaming splinters, run till he nearly expired, be thoroughly beaten again, be beaten nearly to death once more, suffer intolerably in a relationship with a woman, give his consort to Tilopa and watch him maltreat her, and cut off his arms and legs and present them to Tilopa in the form of a mandala. After each of these torments, Tilopa restored him with a touch of his hand and bestowed a precious teaching. The teachings gained in this way, including the renowned six dharmas of Naropa, are those that have been passed down for a millennium in the Kagyu and other lineages.

After further tasks and trials and teachings, finally the transmission of mahamudra through the meeting of the minds took place completely. Tilopa then instructed Naropa to bring benefit to beings. Later, as Tilopa foresaw, Marpa crossed the Himalayas from Tibet, found Naropa, and became his disciple. When Naropa had completed his teachings to Marpa, he prophesied to him that he would have a great spiritual son, Milarepa. At that time, Naropa nodded three times in the direction of Tibet. At the same time all the trees of that region of northern India (Pullahari) bowed three times toward Tibet. They still remain inclined in that direction today.

The Vidyadhara's commentaries on the life of Naropa go far to illuminate the nature of the spiritual path, a subject that is still scarcely understood. In this way they provide a fundamental background for those seeking to fathom his thought. They are especially helpful in explaining why, throughout the nearly twenty years that he taught in the West, he continued to warn against and castigate lukewarm approaches to spirituality that seek to integrate it "reasonably" into conventional life. He decried as spiritual materialism the use of spiritual truths and practices as a means to promote happiness, health, success in society, and other comforts of ego. From the moment Naropa caught a glimpse of the ugly woman, these are precisely the things to which he had to give up his attachment—down to the last trace. Thus, in offering commentary on the life of Naropa, the Vidyadhara can teach us directly of the genuine spirituality—raw and rugged, as he often described it—that he himself abandoned all comforts in order to instill.

SHERAB CHÖDZIN
Nova Scotia, 1992

PART ONE

Life of Naropa Seminar I

NEW YORK 1972

I

Naropa and Us

WE ARE GOING to discuss the life and teachings of Naropa
fully and completely, but not fully and completely in the way
you would like. We are going to discuss the outlines of
Naropa's life and his relationship with his guru Tilopa, and
the twelve acts of repentance he had to go through. We will
also discuss his mahamudra experience. *Mahamudra* means
"great symbol"; it is connected with seeing the phenomena of
the world as they are. We will close our discussion with the
six teachings of Naropa.

I find it necessary to express my negativities about presenting such potent—two hundred percent potent—teachings to
the people of the continent of North America, or to the West
altogether. Nobody here seems to be ready for this material at
all. People are relating with the starting point of practice, and
as far as we know, nobody in America has a complete understanding of even the hinayana level of Buddhism. People have
hardly any understanding at all. They have a completely
schizophrenic attitude: they conceive of a divine, enlightened
personality that is opposed to their confused version of themselves. As a result, people regard themselves as abandoned
people, completely bad people. Or else they might have some
hope, but that again is based on some kind of spiritual pride
that does not leave any leeway for confusion at all. So we're
hopeless. I'm afraid we're hopeless.

Isn't that a terrible, grim picture? Extremely grim. We are

hopeless, absolutely confused. We are so confused we do not even know why we are here listening to this. We wonder why. We are extremely confused, bewildered. What can we do about that? Let alone talking about Naropa?

Naropa achieved something. He found his way in the end. Once he became a disciple of Tilopa, he was okay. But before he became a disciple of Tilopa, he was confused, as much as we are.

Spiritual practice is stepping out of the duality of me-ness and my-ness as opposed to otherness, of who is me and who is not me. But in addition to this we have the further confusion of gurus laying their trips on us. Or, as they are called in America, guh-ROOS. That particular species of human beings we call guh-ROOS are mysterious. They save you. They tell you they save you entirely, but on the other hand they tell you they still have to work on themselves. We are confused. They are broke. It's a hopeless situation.

If we want to write essays about that for our Ph.D., we won't be able to, because we are so confused. Even if we want to become professional gurus, we won't be able to make head or tail of it. Of course a lot of people decide to "make a journey to the East," to live with the natives: study with them, eat with them, and shit with them, whether they use toilet tissue or not. They are serious, obviously, and faithful in playing Burmese games, Japanese games, and so on. They get right into it—sit with the Orientals, eat with them, shit with them. We are getting back a lot of anthropological messages about these "primitive" societies. It seems that though they are primitive, their spiritual understanding is much higher than ours. In any case, these are the trips we have going on.

I would like to call your attention to the following passage from the *Life of Naropa:*

Once when 'Jig-med grags-pa (Abhayakirti) [Naropa],[1] with his back to the sun, was studying the books on grammar, epistemology, spiritual precepts, and logic, a terrifying shadow fell on them. Looking round he saw behind him an old woman with thirty-seven ugly features: her eyes were red and deep-hollowed; her hair was fox-coloured and dishevelled; her forehead large and protruding; her face had many wrinkles and was shrivelled up; her ears were long and lumpy; her nose was twisted and inflamed; she had a yellow beard streaked with white; her mouth was distorted and gaping; her teeth were turned in and decayed; her tongue made chewing movements and moistened her lips; she made sucking noises and licked her lips; she whistled when she yawned; she was weeping and tears ran down her cheeks; she was shivering and panting for breath; her complexion was darkish blue; her skin rough and thick; her body bent and askew; her neck curved; she was hump-backed; and, being lame, she supported herself on a stick. She said to Naropa: "What are you looking into?"

"I study the books on grammar, epistemology, spiritual precepts, and logic," he replied.

"Do you understand them?"

"Yes."

"Do you understand the words or the sense?"

"The words."

The old woman was delighted, rocked with laughter, and began to dance, waving her stick in the air. Thinking that she might feel still happier, Naropa added: "I also understand the sense." But then the woman began to weep and tremble and she threw her stick down.

"How is it that you were happy when I said that
I understood the words, but became miserable when
I added that I also understood the sense?"

"I felt happy because you, a great scholar, did
not lie and frankly admitted that you only understood the words. But I felt sad when you told a lie
by stating that you understood the sense, which you
do not."

"Who, then, understands the sense?"

"My brother."

"Introduce me to him wherever he may be."

"Go yourself, pay your respects to him, and beg
him that you may come to grasp the sense."

With these words, the old woman disappeared
like a rainbow in the sky. [*The Life and Teaching of
Naropa,* trans. Herbert V. Guenther (Boston & London:
Shambhala Publications, 1986), pp. 24–25]

Naropa was studying epistemology, logic, philosophy, and
grammar. That's where we are at. Of course everybody is also
extremely involved with art now. Everybody is trying to work
out their artistic self-expression. They might hear the teachings of Naropa in connection with art; they might see it in
terms of "the art of the Tibetan teachings." Then there is also
logic, the question of how the teachings relate with each
other, how not and how so. We are involved with logic as
well. It could be said that everybody here is in the first stage
of Naropa's experience, involved in philosophy and art, as well
as epistemology. We are on the same level that Naropa was
experiencing before he attained enlightenment. We want an
answer; we want definitions. We want a fixed situation rather
than something fluid. We feel that concepts are very badly
needed.

In this seminar you are not going to be able to relate with

concepts. You're not going to get something out of studying logic, epistemology, grammar, and philosophy—which were a failure for Naropa as well. That is why he had to go through twelve stages of punishment, because of his concepts. We are going to go through the same journey that Naropa went through; we are going to take a tour of Naropa's agony. In some ways, it is going to be like Disneyland. You go through some tunnel, and you come out; you're delivered to somewhere else. You see exciting things and you come out on the other end. But in this case, it is related with psychological problems. It is going to be more deathening, more hellish or heavenish. We start at Naropa's starting point of searching for goodness and trying to achieve divinity.

2

Genuine Madness and Pop Art

And he proceeded onwards in an Eastern direction.

These were the visions he had:

When he had come to a narrow footpath that wound between rocks and a river, he found a leper woman without hands and feet blocking the path.

"Do not block the way, step aside."

"I cannot move. Go round if you are not in a hurry, but if you are, jump over me."

Although he was full of compassion, he closed his nose in disgust and leaped over her. The leper woman rose in the air in a rainbow halo and said:

> Listen, Abhayakirti:
> The Ultimate in which all become the same
> Is free of habit-forming thought and
>   limitations.
> How, if still fettered by them,
> Can you hope to find the Guru?

At this the woman, the rocks, and the path all vanished and Naropa fell into a swoon on a sandy plateau. When he recovered consciousness he thought: "I did not recognize this to be the Guru, now I shall ask anyone I meet for instruction." Then he got up and went on his way praying.

On a narrow road he met a stinking bitch crawling with vermin. He closed his nose and jumped over the animal, which then appeared in the sky in a rainbow halo and said:

> All living beings by nature are one's parents.
> How will you find the Guru, if
> Without developing compassion
> On the Mahayana path
> You seek in the wrong direction?
> How will you find the guru to accept you
> When you look down on others?

After these words the bitch and the rocks disappeared and Naropa again swooned on a sandy plateau.

When he came to, he resumed his prayers and his journey, and met a man carrying a load.

"Have you seen the venerable Tilopa?"

"I have not seen him. However, you will find behind this mountain a man playing tricks on his parents. Ask him."

When he had crossed the mountain, he found the man, who said:

"I have seen him, but before I tell you, help me to turn my parents' head."

But Abhayakirti thought: "Even if I should not find the venerable Tilopa, I cannot associate with a scoundrel, because I am a prince, a Bhikshu, and a scholar. If I seek the Guru I will do so in a respectable way according to the dharma."

Everything happened as before, the man receded into the centre of a rainbow halo and said:

> How will you find the Guru, if
> In this doctrine of Great Compassion
> You do not crack the skull of egotism
> With the mallet of non-Pure-Egoness and
> nothingness?

The man disappeared like a rainbow and Naropa fell senseless to the ground. When he woke up there was nothing and he walked on praying as he went.

Beyond another mountain he found a man who was tearing the intestines out of a human corpse and cutting them up. Asked whether he had seen Tilopa, he answered:

"Yes, but before I show him to you, help me to cut up the intestines of this decayed corpse."

Since Naropa did not do so, the man moved away into the centre of a rainbow-coloured light and said:

> How will you find the Guru, if
> You cut not Samsara's ties
> With the unoriginatedness of the Ultimate
> In its realm of non-reference?

And the man disappeared like a rainbow.

When Naropa had recovered from his swoon and gone on his way praying, he found on the bank of a river a rascal who had opened the stomach of a live man and was washing it with warm water. When he asked him whether he had seen the venerable Tilopa, he replied:

"Yes, but before I show him, help me."

Again Naropa refused, and the man appearing in a centre of light in the sky said:

How will you find the Guru, if
With the water of profound instruction
You cleanse not Samsara, which by nature [is]
    free
Yet represents the dirt of habit-forming
    thoughts?

And the man disappeared in the sky.

After having woken from his swoon Naropa
prayed and journeyed on until he came to the city
of a great king, whom he asked whether he had
seen Tilopa. The king replied:

"I have seen him, but marry my daughter before
I show him to you."

Having taken her, he seemed to spend a long
time. Then the king, not wishing to let him go,
took back the girl and the dowry and left the room.
Not recognizing this as a magic spell, but thinking
that he would have to employ force with the aid of
the *bDe-mchog rtsa-rgyud, Abhidhana-uttaratantra,* he
heard a voice say:

Are you not deceived by a magic show?
How then will you find the Guru
If through desire and dislike you fall
Into the three forms of evil life?

And the whole kingdom disappeared.

When Naropa came to, he travelled in prayer
until he met a dark man with a pack of hounds, a
bow and arrows.

"Have you seen Tilopa?"
"Yes."
"Show him to me."

"Take this bow and arrow and kill that deer."
When Naropa refused, the man said:

> A hunter, I have drawn the arrow
> Of the phantom body which from desires is
>   free
> In the bow, of radiant light the essence:
> I shall kill the fleeing deer of this and that,
> On the mountain of the body believing in
>   an I.
> Tomorrow I go fishing in the lake.

So saying, he disappeared.

When Naropa had recovered he continued prayerfully in search of the Guru and came to the shore of a lake full of fish. Nearby two old people were ploughing a field, killing and eating the insects they found in the furrows.

"Have you seen Tilopa?"

"He stayed with us, but before I show him to you—hallo, wife, come and get this Bhikshu something to eat."

The old woman took some fish and frogs from her net and cooked them alive. When she invited Naropa to eat, he said: "Since I am a Bhikshu I no longer have an evening meal, and besides that I do not eat meat." Thinking, "I must have violated the doctrine of the Buddha to be asked to dine by an old woman who cooks fish and frogs alive," he sat there miserably. Then the old man came up with an ox on his shoulders and asked his wife: "Have you prepared some food for the Bhikshu?" She replied: "He seems to be stupid; I cooked some food, but he said that he did not want to eat."

Then the old man threw the pan into the fire while fish and frogs flew up into the sky. He said:

> Fettered by habit-forming thoughts, 'tis hard
>   to find the Guru.
> How will you find the Guru if you eat not
> This fish of habit-forming thoughts, but
>   hanker
> After pleasures (which enhance the sense of
>   ego)?
> Tomorrow I will kill my parents.

He then disappeared.

After his recovery Naropa came upon a man who had impaled his father on a stake, put his mother into a dungeon, and was about to kill them. They cried loudly: "Oh son, do not be so cruel." Although Naropa was revolted at the sight, he asked the man whether he had seen Tilopa, and was answered: "Help me to kill the parents who have brought me misfortune and I will then show you Tilopa."

But since Naropa felt compassion for the man's parents, he did not make friends with this murderer. Then with the words:

> You will find it hard to find the Guru
> If you kill not the three poisons that derive
> From your parents, the dichotomy of this and
>   that.
> Tomorrow I will go and beg,

the man disappeared.

When Naropa had recovered from his swoon and

gone on in prayer, he came to a hermitage. One of
the inmates recognized him as Abhayakirti and
asked: "Why have you come? Is it to meet us?"

"I am merely a Ku-su-li-pa,[1] there is no need for
a reception."

The hermit, however, did not heed his words and
received him with due honours. Asked for the
reason for his coming, Naropa said: "I seek Tilopa.
Have you seen him?"

"You will find that your search has come to an
end. Inside is a beggar who claims to be Tilopa."

Naropa found him within sitting by the fire and
frying live fish. When the hermits saw this, they
began angrily to beat the beggar, who asked: "Don't
you like what I do?"

"How can we when evil is done in a hermitage?"

The beggar snapped his fingers, said "Lohivagaja,"[2] and the fish returned to the lake. Naropa,
realizing that this man must be Tilopa, folded his
hands and begged for instruction. The Guru passed
him a handful of lice, saying:

> If you would kill the misery of habit-forming
>   thoughts
> And ingrained tendencies on the endless path
> To the ultimate nature of all beings,
> First you must kill (these lice).

But when Naropa was unable to do so, the man
disappeared with the words:

> You will find it hard to find the Guru
> If you kill not the louse of habit-forming
>   thoughts,

Self-originated and self-destructive.
Tomorrow I will visit a freak show.

Dejectedly Naropa got up and continued his search. Coming to a wide plain, he found many one-eyed people, a blind man with sight, an earless one who could hear, a man without a tongue speaking, a lame man running about, and a corpse gently fanning itself. When Naropa asked them if they had seen Tilopa, they declared:

"We haven't seen him or anyone else. If you really want to find him, do as follows:

"Out of confidence, devotion, and cetainty,
    become
A worthy vessel, a disciple with the courage
    of conviction.
Cling to the spirituality of a Teacher in the
    spiritual fold,
Wield the razor of intuitive understanding as
    the viewpoint,
Ride the horse of bliss and radiance as the
    method of attention,
Free yourself from the bonds of this and that
    as the way of conduct.
Then shines the sun of self-lustre which
    understands
One-eyedness as the quality of many,
Blindness as seeing without seeing a thing,
Deafness as hearing without hearing a thing,
Muteness as speaking without saying
    something,
Lameness as moving without being hurried,
Death's immobility as the breeze of the
    Unoriginated (like air moved by a fan).

In this way the symbols of Mahamudra were
pointed out, whereafter everything disappeared."

[Pp. 30–36]

In the teachings proclaimed by the Kagyu lineage, we find
a lot of processes that have to be gone through and understand-
ings that have to be developed. This is by no means easy. It is
extremely difficult to understand that there is some basic
confusion we have created, and that within that confusion
there is also some kind of madness. Strangely enough, the
madness is not confused. There is sanity in the confusion and
the madness. Confusion in dealing with the situation of life as
a fixed thing seems to be a sane approach. So what seems to
be insane is enlightenment.

Naropa's approach to his successive discoveries in his visions—or whatever they are, phantoms that he sees—is connected with his seeming sanity. Because Naropa was born a
prince and was educated and became a professor at Nalanda
University, he regards himself as a sensible person, an educated, sensible person, someone highly respected. But this
sensible quality, this sanity of his, turns out to be a very
clumsy way of relating with the teachings of Tilopa—the
teachings of the Kagyu lineage. Because he was not enough of
a freak, because he was not insane enough, he couldn't relate
with them at all.

Insanity in this case is giving up logical arguments, giving
up concept. Things as they are conceptualized are not things
as they are. We have to try to see within the conceptualized
situation, according to which fire is hot and the sky is blue.
Maybe the sky is green; maybe fire is cold. There's that
possibility, always.

When we hear someone say such a thing we become
extremely perplexed and annoyed. We think: "Of course fire
is hot; fire is not cold. Of course the sky is blue, not green.

That's nonsense! I'm not going to have anything to do with that kind of nonsense. I'm going to stick to my sensible outlook. The sky is blue and fire is hot; that gives me a sense of security, satisfaction, and sanity. If fire is hot, I'm quite happy with it. If the sky is blue, I'm also happy with that. I don't want any interference with my regular line of thought."

On the other hand, the idea of insanity we are looking into here does not mean that you should drop your ordinary sanity and be swinging and hip, to use current conventional terms. I am not saying you should change your entire perspective around, that instead of being clean, you should be dirty because that's a more hip way to behave, or that you should adopt any of the rest of that kind of approach. That is not quite the point. People might think that Naropa's hang-up was that he was not hip enough to experience Tilopa's doctrine or teaching. That is not quite so. There is a problem in communicating this situation to late-twentieth-century Americans. We have an enormous problem there.

One of the biggest problems we face is the popularity of Tibetan Buddhism and Tibetan Buddhist works of art. Everything is regarded as fabulous, a fantastic display. "It is so fantastic! It matches what I saw in my acid trip! It's fabulous!" Looking at it with this attitude, the style of Naropa and his hang-ups and the style of Tilopa and his teachings might be seen as pop art, with people just thinking, "It's a far-out thing." Tibetan wrathful deities in paintings and thangkas demonstrate a crazy-wisdom quality, which is pop art from the point of view of those who regard connecting with the teachings as a hip thing to do.

There are problems with that. Take the example of going into retreat in a cabin in the woods under severe conditions. That should not be regarded as an alternative form of luxury. The retreat cabin you meditate in has nothing to do with your reaction against your central-heated home or your penthouse.

It has nothing to do with that at all. It just provides another life situation, and that's all. Meditating in retreat in a cabin in the remote countryside is not pop art. The same is true for visualizing all kinds of deities and mandalas as some American students have been instructed to do. The first impact on them seems to be: "At last I am able to relate with those beautiful, colorful, groovy things that are in the Tibetan thangkas. At last I have managed to get to relate with that. At last the dream comes true, and I am able to live real pop art. I'm not only thinking of them or painting them; by visualizing, I'm becoming part of them. It's an exciting, outlandish thing to do." It's a kind of pop art.

To come back to Naropa, this seems to be precisely Naropa's hang-up. He had so much fascination about Tilopa and receiving the tantric teachings from him that he also looked at it as the next groovy thing to do. And he walked and walked and walked and went on and on. But at each point he got hit because he regarded the whole thing as pop art according to the conception of that particular age. And it is possible that we ourselves might experience the same kind of situation as well, if we impulsively regard the whole thing as pop art—as colorful, inspiring, and, at the same time, artistic. As long as we regard it as something we might tune into at any time, whenever we like, thinking that as soon as we do, it will relieve us from all our pressures and tensions—as long as we regard it as another escape, another sidetrack—being hit like Naropa could happen to us too.

All the successive situations that Naropa went through in experiencing Tilopa's different qualities—the leper woman, the decaying dog, the criminal, and so on—involve a psychological expectation that is an extremely confused one. And we try to make pictures out of that psychological confusion. And the only kind of picture we can come up with is a beautiful, colorful, artistic kind of picture with a dreamy quality connected with possibly achieving a goal, an aim and object. In other words, our picture is connected with the idea of reaching heaven. That seems to be the problem—because such an idea has nothing to do with truth or reality as the Kagyu lineage speaks of it, nothing to do with the mahamudra experience. Such ideas are not real truth. Bliss is not the real truth. Meditative absorption is not the real truth. It seems the real truth is naked and direct, uncolored, unshaded, and not manufactured—the simple existence of a solitary rock—which seems to be extremely boring to experience. We might think, "If I'm not going to get any excitement or understanding out of experiencing such a truth, what the hell am I getting into this trip for?"

And that seems to be our problem. When we try to get into something, we expect a lot—entertainment, precision, an answer, reassurance, clarity. We expect all kinds of things. By expecting clarity, we are confusing the whole issue; we are producing confusion. By expecting reassurance, by expecting to be reassured that the trip we are getting into is right, we are creating more paranoia. Paranoia and reassurance speak the same language; they're on the same level; they're always interdependent. By looking for precise understanding, we are arousing fear of confusion, we are making more confusion constantly. When we think of bliss, we are making a reference point out of this blissful state, therefore we are arousing fear of pain; we are creating further pain under the pretense of trying to create bliss. These are the things that Naropa experienced in his search for Tilopa. And that is also what we are experiencing. That is what generally happens. We try to grasp every situation of confusion as fast as possible; we grasp it, dwell on it, make it into a mother, suck as much milk as possible out of it, dwell further on it, bounce on it.

In a sense it is beautiful that we can relate to Naropa's confusion as our confusion. It is extremely beautiful that we can relate with him. We can also relate with his understanding. We ourselves could become like Naropa, the father of the Kagyu lineage. This whole room we are in together is filled with potential Naropas, because the whole room is filled with the potentiality of Naropa's confusion. It is quite beautiful.

It seems that in relation to the whole thing we are talking about, Naropa's attainment of enlightenment is not that important. It is Naropa's confusion that is important for us as ordinary people. Connecting with that provides a basis for progress, for a step toward understanding. So let us relate with his story that way. All the hang-ups that Naropa experienced, all his imaginations—his visual mind, his auditory mind as he experienced them—are part of our makeup as well. And there are possibilities of stepping out of that confusion.

STUDENT: I am confused by some of the things Naropa was asked to do. Seemingly there shouldn't be any contradiction between a guru's teaching and the Buddha's teaching. And yet in the visions there seem to be a lot of them. For example, asking him to kill lice seems to be a direct contradiction. On the one hand, his "sane," sensible mind is saying, "Don't do this"; on the other, it is saying, "Do this." It seems either way the poor guy turns, he gets cut down. What would have happened if he had killed the lice? He still would have been in violation, so to speak.

TRUNGPA RINPOCHE: Probably at that moment there was no such thing as lice to be killed. Physically there may have been no lice at all.

S: Still, you're killing, whether it's only a projection or not. If you kill somebody in a dream, isn't that the same as actually carrying out the action?

TR: It's quite different. You're dealing with your own projections in a dream. If you dreamed that you became a million-aire, you wouldn't actually become a millionaire.

S: It still sounds suicidal. Even if the lice aren't there, something exists.

TR: Yes, something exists, which is your projections, your dogma, your resistance, which has to be killed. Of course there is something there; not only something, but *the* thing is there.

S: If it's killed, you're still left a killer aren't you?

TR: Attaining enlightenment could be described as killing ego.

S: It sounds suicidal and hence not complete.

TR: It is complete. When you attain enlightenment, the killer of ego is so efficient and precise that ego cannot arise again at all, not even a memory of it. It does a very fine job. When we kill somebody in the literal sense, we cannot kill them completely. We can't kill their name, we can't kill their relatives—something is left. But in killing ego in connection with the attainment of enlightenment, we do a complete job—the name and the concept are killed as well.

S: Sometimes you talk about meditation in terms of making friends with yourself. Is this what you call making friends with yourself?

TR: What self?

S: It just doesn't seem very friendly.

TR: It is the act of a friend, an act of compassion. Ego is murdered out of compassion, out of love. Usually murder takes place out of hate. It is because the murder of ego is done out of compassion that, quite surprisingly, it is complete. The murder of ego is a complete murder, in contrast to the other kind.

S: Putting it out of its misery.

TR: Not quite. Respecting the misery.

STUDENT: Rinpoche, it sounds as though you're saying we have to go beyond, transcend ego, before we even have the right to get into tantra.

TRUNGPA RINPOCHE: Go beyond? I think we have to, yes. It seems that in the current situation in America, we are in the stage of being haunted by the lady with the thirty-seven ugly marks as Naropa was. We haven't developed to the next stages of Naropa's search for Tilopa at all yet. We have just stayed at the beginning. At the moment we seem to be just discovering the difference between the words and the sense. The discovery of the word seems to be the sense, but that is not quite the case. Discovering the words was what Naropa was doing reading that particular book with his back to the sun. Reading a book on logic. We seem to be at that level. So we have a long way to go.

STUDENT: Is each one of these situations that Naropa goes through a step in developing out of his confusion?

TRUNGPA RINPOCHE: Each situation has a different symbolism related with that, yes.

STUDENT: Who is arranging all these visions?

TRUNGPA RINPOCHE: Nobody. It just seems to happen that way.

STUDENT: Rinpoche, could you say more about the madness or insanity you were talking about?

TRUNGPA RINPOCHE: It is madness beyond the conceptualized point of view of ego. For example, if you are in an outrageous state of hatred and trying to relate with somebody as an object of that hatred, if that person doesn't communicate back to you in terms of hate, you might think he is a mad person. You think he is mad because he doesn't fight you back. As far as you are concerned, that person is mad, because he has lost his perspective of aggression and passion as it should be from the point of view . . .

S: From the point of view of samsara?

TR: Yes. From the point of view of samsara, Buddha is mad. There's a story in the Indian scriptures that in a particular country, a soothsayer predicted to the king that there would be seven days of rain containing a substance that would make people mad. Whoever drank the water would go mad. So his whole kingdom was going to go mad. Hearing this prediction, the king collected gallons and gallons of water for his private use to keep himself from going mad. Then the rain fell and everyone else went mad. Then they all began accusing the king of being mad. Finally he gave in and decided to drink the water of madness in order to fit in with the rest of the kingdom. He couldn't be bothered keeping himself "insane."

STUDENT: In the different visions that Naropa has, he doesn't want to do the things he's asked to do, presumably because he thinks they're immoral. So are we to conclude from this that morality and the moral law are purely something that operates in the ego realm, and that an enlightened person in the position of Tilopa follows no moral law?

TRUNGPA RINPOCHE: Tilopa does follow the moral law in its absolute perfection.

S: What does that mean?

TR: The conventional moral law purely has to do with relating with your conscience rather than dealing with situations. Dealing with situations, with what is right and what is wrong in situations, is Tilopa's fashion. If you relate with a situation in terms of your conscience or your perceptions, it means you don't actually relate with the situation at all; you don't even have any idea of understanding the situation. This seems to be what happens in general in life. You have to try to understand situations as precisely as possible, but there are situations that you regard as bad to understand. For example, if you had to investigate a murder case, you might want to dissociate yourself from the case altogether, thinking, "I don't want to be involved with murder at all." Then you have no way at all of understanding how and why one person murdered the other. You could let yourself become involved with that murder case and try to understand the rightness and wrongness of what was done as scientifically as possible. You could look into the situation in terms of cause and effect and gain some understanding of it. But on the other hand, if you think, "Becoming involved with murder will just get me in contact with bad vibrations, so I'll have nothing to do with that," then you seal yourself off completely.

That is exactly the same thing that seems to be happening in present-day society. Particularly the young generation doesn't want to have anything to do with society—let alone understand it—because it's something ugly, something terrible. This creates tremendous confusion and conflict. Whereas if people were to get into society and try to understand what is wrong, there might be some intelligence coming out of that. Complete rejection without discrimination seems to be the problem.

STUDENT: So should we register to vote?

TRUNGPA RINPOCHE: Why not? Add your energies to the country's.

STUDENT: Don't you think there have been some things

we've all learned from that rejection you were just talking about?

TRUNGPA RINPOCHE: Yes and no—both. A lot of people have rejected Christianity and gone to Hinduism or Buddhism. They feel that they no longer have any associations with Christianity at all. Then later—from the point of view of aliens—they begin to realize that Christianity speaks some kind of profound truth. They only see that from the point of view of aliens, having gone away. They begin to appreciate the culture they were brought up in. Finally they become the best Christians, people with much more understanding of Christianity than ordinary Christians.

You can't reject your history. You can't say that your hair is black if it is blond. You have to accept your history. Those wanting to imitate Oriental culture might go so far as to become 100 percent Hindu or 100 percent Japanese, even to the point of undergoing plastic surgery. But somehow denying your existence—your body, your makeup, your psychological approach—does not help. In fact, it brings more problems. You have to be what you are. You have to relate with your country, the state of your country, its politics, its culture. That is extremely important, since you cannot become someone else. And it is such a blessing.

If we could become someone else, or halfway someone else, that would provide us with a tremendous number of sidetracks and possibilities for escape. We should be thankful that we have a body, a culture, a race, and a country that is honestly ours, and we should relate with those. We can't reject all that. That represents our relationship to the earth as a whole, our national karma, and all the rest of it. That seems to be the starting point for attaining enlightenment, becoming a buddha, an American buddha.

STUDENT: Rinpoche, Naropa's experiences seem to be all

symbols. Can't we go too far in taking everything as a symbol? How do we prevent ourselves from going too far in that sense?

TRUNGPA RINPOCHE: Naropa in a sense failed in this way because he didn't have the chance of relating with Tilopa immediately. For that very reason, he got too much involved in symbolism. The same could apply to us as well. It's not so much a matter of too much symbolism as of too much fascination with the context. For example, you could be completely fooled by a salesman if you're in a shop. The salesman might say, "This is such beautiful material. This is such a functional item. It's of good quality, yet cheap. It's so beautiful; you'll be getting your money's worth." At that point, you can't deny that what the salesman is telling you is the truth. He's absolutely telling the truth. The thing he's trying to sell you does have those good qualities. But if you ended up buying it on the basis of fascination, you might be disappointed afterward, because somehow afterward you're not relating with it on the same level of fascination anymore. You might find at that point that your fascination is rejected by the experience you had in your first glimpse before the salesman began to fascinate you. The whole thing is based on fascination.

S: What I was asking about was if there was a point where one has gone too far in taking experiences as symbolic, a point where the whole thing's a projection.

TR: Yes, that is related with fascination, not being able to relate with yourself. One has to relate to one's whole being rather than just purely dealing with accuracy and beautiful display.

STUDENT: In the Buddhist tradition, after the death of ego, is there any self left? Does self exist?

TRUNGPA RINPOCHE: That's a very old question. You see,

in order to have the continuity of something, you have to have somebody constantly watching this continuity happening. If you have ego continuing, you also have to have the observer observing that ego is continuing. This is because the whole thing is based on a mirage. If there's no watcher, there's no mirage. If there's a watcher to acknowledge that the mirage exists, there will be a mirage. After enlightenment, there's no watcher anymore; therefore the watcher's object does not exist anymore.

S: Does the being exist after that?

TR: The being is self-consciousness, making sure you are there. And you don't watch yourself being there anymore. It's not a question of whether being exists or does not exist. If you see being as not existing, then you have to watch that, make sure that being does not exist anymore, which is continuing the being anyhow.

S: So in other words, there is a death or an identity after ego death, and the death of ego is the death of confusion about it?

TR: Well, the watcher dissolves, so we cannot say yes or no either. It's beyond remark.

STUDENT: Regarding relating with our culture, Alan Watts says that one thing that has given our culture a great neurosis is seeing things in terms of the conflict between good and evil rather than just seeing them as they are. This makes me want to ask you about the Buddhist view of what the devil is or the black magician. A lot of our cultural history that is still going on has to do with black magic.

TRUNGPA RINPOCHE; Defining good and evil or the devil and black magic is very much related to our topic of sanity and insanity, and the whole subject of meditation is related with that as well. The result of any situation that is connected with self-enrichment, or an attempt at self-perpetuation, either in an ego-centered way or a very innocent and kind way—the result of anything aimed at enriching the ego—is destruction, complete confusion, perpetual confusion. There is no killing of ego here. From a black magician's point of view, you don't kill somebody's ego, you kill somebody's non-ego.

S: How can you do that?

TR: You just do it out of conviction, belief. In other words you can't destroy it completely, but you put a smear of ink over it, and you don't look again; you just hope for the best—that you killed it. The whole thing is connected with spiritual materialism, which I talk so much about. Spiritual materialism means enriching the ego. Anything related with spiritual materialism is a step toward the black magician, if I may say so. It could be a step toward the black magician or the white magician actually, but in any case toward the magician, toward gaining power. If you want to help your friend, you just do it. If you want to destroy your enemy, you just do it. In that way, you have the potential of the black magician, even if you are regarded as a kind person who is at the same time a powerful person.

The whole question is how much the relationship with ego becomes a central theme in spiritual practice. When it does, you get good and bad, what is and what is not, which is called duality in Buddhist terminology. The whole thing of who you are is purely related with the watcher. You can't measure anything without a starting point. And you can't count unless you can start from zero. So zero is you, ego. You start from there and you build your number series, you build your measurement system, you build your relationships. Once you do that, you get an overwhelming sense of good and kind or bad and destructive. You build all kinds of things based on that basic reference point. It seems that the whole thing is based on how much you are involved with ego. That seems to be the basis for defining goodness or wickedness.

STUDENT: What are the methods in your way for killing the ego? What methods would you use in our society?

TRUNGPA RINPOCHE: It has nothing to do with society at all. It is purely a matter of dealing with one's psychological state of being. Sociological styles don't make any difference in this regard. Sociological approaches or styles are just a photograph. The direct way of dealing with ourselves here is getting into the nitty gritty of our whole existence and dealing with excruciating pain and excruciating pleasure as directly as possible. That way we begin to realize that pain and pleasure do not exist in a centralized way, but pain and pleasure exist in an expansive, joyful way. So we don't have to nurse anything.

STUDENT: Rinpoche, you spoke of compassion as being bad medicine for ego. Yet Naropa violates our definition of compassion in a number of ways.

TRUNGPA RINPOCHE: There are two different types of compassion. There is actual compassion, direct compassion, absolute compassion. Then there is the other kind of compassion that Mr. Gurdjieff[3] calls idiot compassion, which is compassion with neurosis, a slimy way of trying to fulfill your desire secretly. This is your aim, but you give the appearance of being generous and impersonal.

S: What is absolute compassion?

TR: Absolute compassion is seeing the situation as it is, directly and thoroughly. If you have to be tough, you just do it. In other words, idiot compassion contains a sort of opium—constantly trying to be good and kind—and absolute compassion is more literal, more discriminating, and more definite. You are willing to hurt somebody, even though you do not want to hurt that person; but in order to wake that person up, you might have to hurt him or her, you might have to inflict pain.

That is precisely why, in the Buddhist tradition, we don't start with the teaching of compassion, the mahayana, but we start with teaching of the lesser vehicle, the hinayana. In the hinayana you try to get yourself together. Then you start applying your compassion after that, having gotten yourself together, having built the foundation. You can't just work on the level of absolute compassion right from the beginning. You have to develop toward it.

STUDENT: I think you said earlier that one of the obstacles to developing in this way is the need for reassurance. How does one get away from the need for reassurance?

TRUNGPA RINPOCHE: Acknowledge needing reassurance, acknowledge it as an effigy that looks in only one direction and does not look around. An effigy with one face, possibly only one eye. Doesn't see around, doesn't see the whole situation. Do you see what I mean?

S: The effigy only looks one way. Is this the person who needs reassurance?

TR: Yes, because that reassurance has to be attached to that one situation. Whenever you need reassurance, that means you have a fixed idea of what ought to be. And because of that you fix your vision on one situation, one particular thing. And those situations that are not being observed because of the point of view of needing reassurance, that we are not looking at, are a source of paranoia. We wish we could cover the whole ground, but since we can't do that physiologically, we have to try to stick to that one thing as much as we can. So the need for reassurance has only one eye.

S: And the way to get beyond that one-eyed vision?

TR: Develop more eyes, rather than just a unidirectional radar system. You don't have to fix your eye on one thing. You can have panoramic vision, vision all around at once.

STUDENT: Something like a fish-eye lens.

TRUNGPA RINPOCHE: Something like that, but even that has a camera behind it.

3

An Operation without Anesthetics

NAROPA'S EXPERIENCE OF discovering Tilopa is connected with finally giving up hope, giving up hope of getting what we wanted to get. For Naropa, finally that search for an ultimate answer had to be given up. But this is not easy to give up, because each time we try to give up having the ultimate answer—our final answer, the truth—giving up the truth is discovered as another truth. So we could go on and on and on giving up truths. Giving up hope becomes another hope of getting something out of giving up hope.

We seem to love ourselves enormously. We love ourselves so much that we reach the point where we might kill ourselves. A kind of love-hate relationship goes on in which our extreme desire, our extreme love of ourselves, becomes hatred in practice. This is precisely why samsaric mind, the samsaric point of view of gaining happiness, is regarded by the Buddhist teaching as holding the wrong end of the stick. That is precisely why confusion is regarded as off.

Looking at Naropa's situation, we see that to have found a teacher like Tilopa, we have to give up our conceptualized way of thinking and our conceptualized attitudes. We have to learn that lesson: to become tired of the dreams, sick of them. The dreams have no root. They are purely fantasies. But then, after that, when the dreams cease to function, there is something else to relate with. That is the shell of the dreams. The shell, or the shadow, of the dreams becomes tough and strong. Having woken up, we face reality.

Having given up hope of meeting Tilopa, Naropa finally meets Tilopa. But that turns out to be another problem. That is another uneasy situation. Having gone through the fantasies and used them up, we are faced with the reality or ultimate truth, or whatever you would like to call it. What do we do with the reality? How shall we handle this reality? Having woken up, what shall we do?

A lot of the great Tibetan teachers talk about transcending the phantom of mind and facing reality. Once one faces it, reality is like pure gold. One has to examine that gold, process it—hammer it and mold out of it whatever shapes one wants. Or we could also say that when one faces reality, it is like dough, and processing it is like kneading dough. If you want good bread, you have to knead the dough with complete strength. And it is said that the important point in this is not kneading the dough but cleaning the bowl. If you are good at kneading, you clean the bowl with the dough. The result might be good bread, but this is still uncertain.

Dealing with reality is an extremely big problem, a much bigger one than dealing with the phantoms of our imagination. In our meditation practice, dealing with thought processes is relatively simple. You just relate with thoughts as thoughts, and the thought process becomes transparent. But dealing with the technique of meditation is another matter; dealing with your body is another matter. That is the most difficult problem of all.

Dealing with reality is difficult because we are still approaching it in an unrealistic way. There is reality in its full glory. Should we look at it as a spectrum? Should we regard it as something that belongs to us? Should we regard it as a show? If we don't regard it in any way at all, how are we going to deal with that reality in its full splendor? In fact we do not know what to do with reality. Having been presented with it, we are completely bewildered.

It's like meeting your favorite film star on the street. If you suddenly bumped into him or her on the street, you would have to make up your mind what to say, what to do. Somehow it's a dream coming true; it's real. There is something real about meeting that particular person, but at the same time there is something unreal because you are not prepared for that reality. It happened by accident.

Meeting reality usually takes the form of an accident. We are bewildered by this accident, by this accidental discovery of reality, and then we are uncertain what to do. Should we pull it, push it, possess it, play with it, or what? But actually we don't have to do anything with it. Just let that reality be there. And that seems to be the problem that Naropa encountered in his meeting with Tilopa. He regarded himself as a student and thought he had to do something—ask for Tilopa's teaching. Thus he was still seeing Tilopa as an external person rather than as a part of his own psychological makeup presenting itself as Tilopa.

Dealing with spiritual masters is very tricky. They may be individual persons with a name and age and so on, born in such-and-such a place, with a particular lifestyle. Yet such a master is part of your ghost, part of your shadow; he's your phantom, coming back because you would like to deal with him on the level of spirituality rather than in terms of ego's language.

If you try to deal with him directly in terms of ego's language, it is very, very complicated. Dealing with a lawyer or a salesman is quite simple. If it's a salesman, you just examine the merchandise and pay him money, take your merchandise, and go home. That's a very realistic relationship. But with a spiritual friend it is quite different. You can't pay him with material objects. You can't pay him by being ingratiating or by being aggressive and insisting on getting something out of him: "If you don't teach me, I'll kill you." That doesn't work either. Somehow there is always a very subtle relationship involved. Although there is some kind of exchange, that exchange is very subtle, almost bewildering. And most of us do not know how to relate with it.

Even, Naropa, for instance, didn't know how to relate with it. Naropa was one of the world's most educated men, one of the world's most intelligent scholars. As a professor, Naropa was often referred to as "the only eye of the world." Still, something did not work in the way he dealt with Tilopa. In spite of his scholastic, philosophical, and metaphysical understanding of the dharma, somehow something didn't click at all. In fact, things went the opposite way altogether.

It seems that the relationship between the student and the teacher is a very subtle relationship, and if that subtle relationship does not work, then it works its way into a very painful process. We cannot present ourselves in that subtle relationship as a friend. We have to reduce ourselves to a patient, a sick person. We could be a friend at the same time, but still our main style of presenting ourselves to our spiritual friend is as a physically or mentally fucked-up person—rather than just a friend who is gracious, intelligent, friendly, and loving. Someone might try to present himself that way, but somehow his whole way of carrying his being makes it very difficult for the spiritual friend to accept him in this role of friend.

As a spiritual friend, you see this person inviting himself onto your doorstep. He is frantically shivering, shaking, freaking. Obviously, you invite him in, give him a seat, calm him down. And then you find out what is wrong with this person. Does this person need an operation, or would just some instant medicine help? Usually the person needs an operation more than hospitality.

This operation has different stages. To begin with, one has

to deal with the body and the environment. (When I say "body," I am referring to mind-body.) The whole problem of this person who has come to you, the kind of sickness he has, is a conflict between "that" and "this." "That," in this case, refers to the projections we put out. When we put out projections, they bounce back on us, manifesting as seductive or threatening, or whatever. "This" is the perceiver of those projections.

So there is a conflict between "that" and "this" constantly, all the time. That is the cause of the symptoms of the sicknesses of all kinds that the person who has come to us is going through—all kinds of suffering. It is a sickness of cosmic chaos, a sickness of cosmic misunderstanding, a sickness of losing ground either here or there, losing the ground of "that" or losing the ground of "this." Therefore, the operation is not so much one of cutting out pieces of sickness and sewing the person back up. That doesn't cure. Cutting out the areas of sickness and sewing him back up doesn't mean anything. He still has the sickness; he still has the body.

The only operation that the spiritual friend can perform is a mutual operation. The student should not be under anesthetics of any kind. No anesthetics. It is the experience of the operation that is important rather than the operation itself. A mother might want to have natural childbirth because she wants to see her child being born, brought out of her. She doesn't want to be put under anesthetics. She wants to take part in the whole process of the birth. Here it is exactly the same: we have to have a natural operation rather than one with anesthetics.

And of course every penetration of the knife that cuts the tense skin, full of muscular tension that has developed from the chaos, from the conflict between "this" and "that," is enormously powerful. This tension is just about to explode; that is why the operation is needed. No matter how gentle the physician is, there will be pain. In fact, the gentler the physician, the more acute the pain will be, because the physician does not take any chances. He does not just chop something off, but he is deliberate, very slow and very careful. The stroke of his knife is a very slow movement, extremely slow and kind.

This is exactly the kind of operation that Tilopa performed on Naropa. His operating knife is extremely sharp. At the beginning you hardly notice its cut, but sometime later it becomes overwhelming. That kind gesture, which we talked about earlier as the absence of idiot compassion, is part of dealing with reality, the absolute quality of the world.

It seems that we do not have the time and space here to go into the symbolism of the twelve successive situations that Naropa faced. Each one contains a different symbolism. But we can describe the whole process that those twelve experiences make up. To begin with, it is a process of cutting and opening up, releasing the tension in the skin. The skin is extremely tense because there is pressure from inside and pressure from outside. The inside pressure is confusion and uncertainty about how to relate with things. The external pressure comes from the fact that things we have put out have begun to bounce back on us. There is this extraordinary pressure that builds up, so we cut open the patient's skin and remove a certain part of his organism that is producing this neurological pressure.

This seems to describe the subtle level of the twelve experiences Naropa went through. In this process, the first thing is dealing with the facade, then dealing with the inner phenomena, and then dealing with the innermost ones, going deeper, deeper, deeper into social situations, emotions, and so on. To begin with, there are social hesitations of all kinds that are based on conventional rules. Naropa has been brought up as a prince, and he has an upper-class snobbishness. In accordance with this, his life is based on the expectation that everything will be conducted properly and precisely. That kind of gentility in him is connected with the social setup.

Then there are the inner phenomena, which you get into at the level of being just about to give up social jargon. There is conflict, because it is hard to tune into that inward way of thinking and that inward emotion. This also involves giving up the philosophical and metaphysical beliefs of all kinds that Naropa had acquired.

Then beyond that is naked emotion, direct emotional states.

In other words, these twelve experiences that Naropa went through were a continuous unlearning process. To begin with, he had to unlearn, to undo the cultural facade. Then he had to undo the philosophical and emotional facade. Then he had to step out and become free altogether. This whole process was a very painful and very deliberate operation.

This does not apply to Naropa and his time alone. This could also be something very up to date. This operation is applicable as long as we have conflicting emotions and erroneous beliefs about reality. Conflicting emotions and wrong beliefs about reality are known as the two veils. As long as they remain universal, the treatment, the operation without anesthetics, remains very up to date. And that is merely the beginning.

STUDENT: Are there several layers of emotional veils, different kinds of emotions constituting more than one layer of the veil of conflicting emotions?

TRUNGPA RINPOCHE: According to Nagarjuna's analysis of human psychology, there is the actual emotion, the direct one that we usually call emotion; then there is the intention of that emotion, of that confusion of emotion; and then there is the activator of the emotion. You see, the whole thing goes back to ego's basic formula of maintaining itself. The ego cannot maintain itself unless there is a subtle way of setting its wheels in motion. Those wheels are set into motion by a slight move; then they roll faster, then finally extremely fast. It's like setting anything in motion: first it's slow, then it's faster, then it's extremely fast.

The layers of emotion begin with fascination. There is the fascination with a feeling that there might be something there, but on the other hand there might not—that kind of uncertainty about something's being there. Then one begins to get much more adventurous: "Supposing there is something there, let's look for it, or let's get into it." The whole thing moves more rhythmically. And since there is now something you can move, that you have put forward, then finally you are not only just concerned with that movement or that speed, not just concerned with discovery alone, but you begin to be concerned about what comes after the discovery and begin hoping there will be another discovery. And so on and so on.

So the final emotional state is not so much just wanting to have experience of one thing, but wanting to experience the next thing. So the whole process becomes very fast, very speedy.

STUDENT: You were talking about projecting something out and getting it back and the whole thing reflecting some kind of cosmic chaos. I didn't follow that.

TRUNGPA RINPOCHE: When you project something out, that projection also becomes a message for the next thing. If you shout, your echo comes back to you. If you talk to somebody, that person reacts to your communication. If you put out any vibrations, they automatically rebound back on you. This is a natural thing, which is always there. Scientifically, things happen that way. Because of that, there is the natural situation that it is hard to strategize the whole process. How to deal with the rebounds is the inner level. For that you have to develop another tactic, another policy. Having put something out in the first place was impulse, an impulsive move. But getting what you put out back is an unexpected thing. You will have to work out how to deal with that thing. There's that kind of red tape. Somebody has to be manufacturing foreign policy, so to speak, which makes everything very centralized and self-conscious.

STUDENT: How do you relate to your spiritual friend while you are slowly being cut up by him? You said aggression doesn't work. That seems to be obvious. Various social games don't work. Yet there is this exquisite torture. I suppose that should produce feelings of gratitude, but somehow . . .

TRUNGPA RINPOCHE: Well, you see, he is not dealing with your problems other than through your reactions. Do you see what I mean?

S: No.

TR: The operation is performed on your reactions, not on anything else. Your reactions are the very juicy substance that is cut up and sewn and pieced together. That way you have no room at all to play with, even in the most vague situations like those in the first portion of Naropa's search, before he met Tilopa. Each time he first meets a situation, he has a reaction against it, which triggers off the next situation automatically. And later on there is always a message coming through to him, saying things like, "Tomorrow I will visit a freak show." There is a hint. He blindly keeps failing to guess the message, but he reacts to it.

S: If you could control your reactions, would that help? If your reactions weren't so much in conflict with the situation around you or weren't so aggressive toward it, there wouldn't be that friction. . . .

TR: It's not a question of what you should be or what you

should be doing. It's a question of what you are. The operation can always be performed on what your potential for reactions is. I mean, you can't escape.

STUDENT: Is it right, then, to say that there must be a fundamental trust in your spiritual friend so that you can allow yourself to react however you're going to, knowing that there is a communication that goes beyond your immediate reactions?

TRUNGPA RINPOCHE: I suppose that's the situation. But at the same time that you have a feeling of fundamental, absolute trust, you also have the feeling that you don't want to walk out of the situation while it's still such a mess. You have started already, so your fate is inevitable. It's an unfinished karmic situation.

STUDENT: I didn't quite follow that part about having to relate with your body. Is it that when you see something new, you don't know what to do with it, so you move into a state where you have to relate more with your body than your thoughts? I didn't understand that point.

TRUNGPA RINPOCHE: Well, the starting point is the physical situation. Usually physical problems bring about the fundamental situations leading to meeting the spiritual friend. For example, Naropa's attempt to commit suicide brought Tilopa there. Because finally Naropa is actually relating with his body; finally he has come to the point where the only solution is relating with the earth. Of course, his particular solution was rather a questionable one.

S: I took that symbolically as the suicide of ego.

TR: Yes, but then you are holding the wrong end of the stick by taking the ego to be body rather than mind. There is a confusion as to what really is ego and what is not. You just think, "If I eliminate this tiresome object that gets in the way all the time . . ." But if you eliminate that, you may have no further opportunity of receiving teaching.

In fact what hangs around and gets in the way is ego rather than the body. But still, relatively speaking, that was an intelligent move on the part of confused Naropa. He was beginning to get some sense of the symbolism of ego. But he related to that symbolism by seeing the body as ego. That was the only thing available at the time, which is understandable. For example, if people begin feeling claustrophobic sitting in their offices, they might try to open the window or remove a picture from the wall or something else of that nature. At least that's an intelligent gesture symbolically. But it doesn't really help.

STUDENT: You were talking about the emotion, the intention of the emotion, and then a third thing that I didn't understand.

TRUNGPA RINPOCHE: Those are the stages of the development of the emotion. There's the emotion, the intention, and then the possibility of discovering something, which is inquisitive mind. You start with inquisitive mind and then set things in motion, and then that motion becomes more adventurous. Then finally you not only care about discovering, but you care more about the next thing. Getting something is no longer the answer, but getting something more is the answer, which is based again on the inquisitive mind that was there at the beginning. The Tibetan word for the development of inquisitive mind is *gyuwa*, which means a sort of a flicker. It's like a very bright flashlight. While looking with the flashlight, you don't know what is happening. You close your eyes because of this glaring light, but then you move all the faster with your delayed reaction after the light is off. The occurrence is gyuwa, the impulsive moment of fascination, which is much faster than your reaction. It sees the flashlight beam on this brilliant moment, and then tries to catch the next one, the next moment.

STUDENT: Don't you outpace yourself that way?

TRUNGPA RINPOCHE: Somehow you don't, actually. You make up for the loss of time. A very efficient administrator is running the whole show there.

All the emotions have that kind of starting point of a sudden manipulative, impulsive move. In other words, you can't have emotions at all without an object for putting out your greed or hate or other emotion onto. Then, when you put that emotion out, automatically you get something back. Then you use what you get back as source material for putting out something further. It acts as a kind of fuel. You go on and on like that. When you put out something, you get your fuel back, then you use that fuel for the next one. You build up this whole context.

STUDENT: Could you explain the meaning of Tilopa's repeated formula about how "this body believing in an I" deserves to be gotten rid of, and how Naropa should "look into the mirror of his mind"?

TRUNGPA RINPOCHE: In other words, the ego is the ideal fuel, the fuel that is exciting to burn. Consuming the ego as fuel, that would make a nice fire. If you want to make a good fire, one that is dry and puts out a lot of heat, and doesn't leave a lot of cinders, from the point of view of non-ego, ego is *the* best fuel that could be found in the whole universe. Discovering this delightful fuel, this highly efficient fuel, is based on looking into the mirror of your mind. That is what watches the ego burning. The mirror of your mind, you could say, is one's innate nature or buddha mind, or whatever you would like to call it. It has a very intelligent and extremely practical and scientific quality behind it. So if you look into the mirror of the mind, which sees a panoramic vision of everything, you know how to choose your next fuel of ego.

That is the whole idea of using samsaric situations as stepping stones to enlightenment. And it's also the same idea that if there is no samsara, there is no enlightenment. The two are interdependent.

STUDENT: You're saying that the operation is only a success if the patient dies.

TRUNGPA RINPOCHE: Yes, yes.

STUDENT: In that case, what good does the operation do?

TRUNGPA RINPOCHE: It's a feast, a celebration.

STUDENT: You talked about how the process of projection tends to escalate. It seems there could be two approaches to doing something about it. Either you could de-escalate slowly or attempt to stop cold. Which is the better approach, the one that will work?

TRUNGPA RINPOCHE: To begin with, you don't have to regard the projections as something wrong, something bad you should get rid of. This is precisely the point about ego being the only fuel for wisdom. So projections are welcomed; one is delighted to find projections to work on. One doesn't have to try to shut them off or shut them out, but should take advantage of their presence.

S: How?

TR: By understanding or realizing or appreciating their presence. That appreciation is necessary, of course. If there's appreciation, then obviously the projections won't become demonic or irritating or destructive at all.

STUDENT: How do we arrange to appreciate them?

TRUNGPA RINPOCHE: That probably needs more practice. You don't deliberately try to appreciate them. That doesn't seem to be a particularly accurate way of enjoying oneself. If you feel you have to enjoy something—suppose you felt you had to enjoy a party given by your rich uncle—that doesn't mean you will actually enjoy it. Instead you must just see the factual situations of projections as they are. You don't have to do anything with them. If you don't try to do anything with them, the discoveries come naturally; you have a natural situation there.

STUDENT: Is not trying correlated with a bodily state of relaxation?

TRUNGPA RINPOCHE: Not necessarily. It's actually not trying to do anything at all [even relax]. That's the whole point.

STUDENT: Rinpoche, concerning these twelve tortures, I guess you could call them, that Naropa was put through, I can see that the first one took an incredible amount of courage—or trust or faith. But then he was healed. And each time after that, he was healed. Wouldn't that give the whole thing more of a game quality? Like jumping off a cliff isn't really jumping off a cliff if you know your guru's going to put you back together afterward. So that seems to be cheating a bit.

TRUNGPA RINPOCHE: You have to take into account the extreme and constant sincerity of Naropa. He was a very sincere person. Each time he saw one of those visions, for instance; I mean, by the end of the visions one would expect he would begin to presume there was some message involved. But he was too sincere with himself. He took everything seriously.

S: But he was killed at one time and then revived. I mean, a person has got to notice that!

TR: But still his mind doesn't work that way. The reality is too real for him.

STUDENT: You talked about our dreams and fantasies and said that when those are gone, there is still the shadow of the dreams. What are the shadows?

TRUNGPA RINPOCHE: The shadows are the reality. The shadows of dreams are reality. Dreams are such an insubstantial thing. But that insubstantial thing presents such solid things as its shadow—like a shell. An experience of the shadow of the outer dream experience is meeting Tilopa, the shadow of the dream. Dreams produce reality; reality produces dreams.

S: But when we dream, that's fantasy, not reality.

TR: But the impact of the dream is reality. Our thought process could be called a dream; what happens in our daily life situations is a fantasy as well.

S: So fantasies are useful?

TR: They could be a hang-up at the same time.

S: How do you distinguish whether they're useful or destructive?

TR: You don't have to, particularly. That's the whole problem. When we begin to do that, the whole thing becomes very methodical, too definite, too predictable to be true.

S: So what do you do?

TR: You just float along.

STUDENT: From that point of view, how do you regard the difference between reality and unreality? Or is there any difference?

TRUNGPA RINPOCHE: Well, there seems to be something. I suppose reality is that which is connected with body when you are awake. And unreality is that which is purely connected with your fantasies when you are asleep or when you are in a discursive thought process.

S: Can your fantasies make some impact on your realities? Can some fantasy make you do something real?

TR: That's exactly what I'm saying. The fantasy produces a shell, which is reality. The shadow of the fantasy is reality.

STUDENT: What's the difference between appreciation and fascination?

TRUNGPA RINPOCHE: Fascination works purely in terms of highlights. In other words, appreciation deals with qualities, and fascination deals with the colors of the qualities. One is fascinated by the deep gold quality of gold rather than appreciating gold as something rich and valuable. Fascination is purely involved with the color of gold; appreciation appreciates its value.

S: Fascination is more on the surface.

TR: More on the surface, yes. It's an impulsive thing.

S: You're kind of caught . . .

TR: Caught by the highlights, yes.

STUDENT: You seemed to say that it wasn't necessary to discriminate between useful and destructive fantasies. Is it not necessary to be cautious about the kind of experiences we want to enter into? Don't I have to be concerned about the price I'm paying for an experience? Is there karma?

TRUNGPA RINPOCHE: There's karma always, whatever you do.

S: Then if certain things make more karma, should we avoid entering into those things?

TR: That just creates another karma. Boycotting something also creates karma, as much as taking part in it does.

S: Not less or more?

TR: It's more or less the same, you see, unless the whole process is regarded in terms of the fundamental principle of the creator of the karmic situation. It seems that the practice of meditation is the only way one can step out of planting further karma. Meditation practice has this particular quality of providing a pure gap and not feeding on concepts of any kind. You just deal with the technique. Meditation practice is the only way of providing a gap, of not sowing a further seed. If you're trying to be careful, that also sows a seed. It's almost the same. We could speak in terms of black karma or white karma, but both are a color.

S: Don't certain experiences make it more difficult for us to meditate?

TR: That depends on the context you provide for them, on the way you treat that situation. Some people find complicated or rich surroundings more conducive to meditation. Some people find simple surroundings more conducive.

S: Don't the activities I engage in during the day color my experience when I sit down to meditate?

TR: That depends on how you view them.

S: In a very screwed-up way.

TR: If you view them as something . . .

S: Bad.

TR: . . . bad, that begins to haunt you. If you view something as being extremely good, that also begins to haunt you. The conceptual mind is extremely powerful. It runs the whole show of samsara.

STUDENT: Meditation, then, is the only thing that in and of itself has no color, and therefore . . .

TRUNGPA RINPOCHE: It's at least a primordial gesture. Meditation is a primordial gesture.

4

Something Very Tickling

WHEN NAROPA FINALLY discovered Tilopa, there was no particular gracious occasion. There was no ceremonial initiation of any kind. The initiation consisted in Tilopa's taking off his slipper and slapping Naropa on the cheek, which sent Naropa into a coma, weakened as he was. Then Tilopa sang a song to the effect of "Whatever I have experienced in the mahamudra, Naropa has also experienced, so in the future, whoever is open to the teaching of mahamudra should get it from Naropa."

That was quite interesting and shocking. Naropa achieved realization in a sudden glimpse. But we shouldn't be too optimistic, thinking that we too will experience a sudden transmission like that. Probably we won't. The whole thing is very haphazard, very much a matter of taking a chance.

The teachings of Naropa are known as the six dharmas or six doctrines. The first doctrine connected with his sudden discovery of the mahamudra experience is called illusory body. He discovered that every situation or experience is illusory, is to be regarded as body and nonbody, substance and nonsubstance. He experienced life as like a mirage.

The second doctrine has to do with dream. Our fantasies are involved with trying to pin down experience as something fixed, which actually doesn't exist at all.

Then there is the doctrine related with the bardo experience, which is the intermediate situation between death and birth.

Then we have inner heat, or *tumo,* which in Sanskrit is *chandali,* an inner burning that arouses the universal flame that burns away all conceptualized notions of whatever kind, totally consuming them.

Then there is transference of consciousness. Since you do not believe in physical existence as a solid thing that you can take refuge in, you can switch out of such a belief into nonbelief, transfer your consciousness into open space, a space which has nothing to do with the fixed notion of "me and mine" and "that and this" at all.

The last, the sixth doctrine, is luminosity, *ösel* in Tibetan, all-pervading luminosity. There is nothing at all that is regarded as a dark corner, an area of mystery anymore. The whole thing is seen as open, brilliant, as things as they really are. There are no mysterious corners left.

Very crudely, those are the six doctrines of Naropa. I look forward to a situation in which we have time to go into them in a more subtle and fundamental way. That would be extremely good. At this point I hope we have at least started something in terms of arousing inquisitive mind. There may be something happening somewhere underneath human confusion, which is very tickling.

Let's leave it at that for now and dedicate our actions here, our working together, to American karma. Something is trying to come out of American karma. It's dying to burst, dying to blast. Let's make a homemade bomb out of this seminar.

PART TWO

Life of Naropa Seminar II

KARMÊ-CHÖLING 1973

Pain and Hopelessness

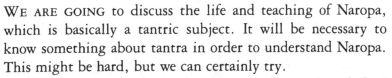

WE ARE GOING to discuss the life and teaching of Naropa, which is basically a tantric subject. It will be necessary to know something about tantra in order to understand Naropa. This might be hard, but we can certainly try.

Tantra, or vajrayana, is the most fundamental and final stage of the development of wisdom in Buddhism. It is the final development of the enlightenment experience. The enlightenment experience has three levels. There is the *nirmanakaya* level, the level of manifestation. On this level, enlightened mind can communicate with ordinary living beings. Then there is the *sambhogakaya* level, the level that communicates with the emotions and energy of ordinary beings. And then there is the *dharmakaya* level, the wisdom that communicates with the greater depths of ignorance in ordinary sentient beings.

Those three types of buddhas are fully dealt with in tantra. It could be said that they are dealt with in the mahayana too, but the final development of the mahayana state is the tantric state. In other words, there is really no such thing as a mahayana buddha. All the buddhas are fully realized, fully awakened in the tantric fashion. That is to say, advanced mahayana becomes tantra.

In the hinayana, enlightened beings are called *arhats*. An arhat is a relatively realized person, who can relate to himself but cannot fully relate with other beings. He understands himself, and consequently he is able to demonstrate the teachings and give the teachings to others. People manage to relate to his understanding of himself, and they in turn develop understanding. This is the learning situation relating with arhats.

However, at this point we are going to discuss the vajrayana, tantra, the ultimate experience of realization. We have to understand the basics of tantra. The way to approach tantra is by developing intellect and intuition, mind and body, so that they work together. Mind and body consciousness working together at the beginner's level means the realization of pain and suffering—having hang-ups and realizing them, having pain and noticing it. This is a very basic level. Still, it requires a certain amount of intelligence.

You might say that it is very easy to understand or experience pain. Oh no. It takes a lot of understanding to realize pain. This level of understanding is what is necessary to prepare the ground for tantra. The tantric type of intelligence exists right at the beginning at the ordinary level, the level of pain. So we shouldn't jump the gun and try to be too advanced, to bypass the ground floor and go right to the top floor. At this point, tantric intelligence is understanding, realizing, experiencing pain.

The term *tantra* means "continuity." It refers to a continuity of intelligence that goes on constantly. This kind of intelligence cannot be inhibited or prevented, and it cannot be interrupted. From the Buddhist point of view our basic being is fundamental intelligence and wakefulness that has been clouded over by all kinds of veils and obscurations. What prevents us from seeing pain is that we fail to see these veils. The method used in tantra to enable us to realize pain is called *mantra*.

In this case mantra has nothing to do with some verbal gibberish that you repeat over and over. Mantra here is an *upaya,* a skillful means. The derivation of the word *mantra* is the Sanskrit *mantraya,* which is a combination of two words. *Manas* means "mind," and *traya* means "protection." So mantra protects the mind, the fundamental intelligence or wakefulness. It does not protect it by using guards or putting it under a glass dome. Protection here is clearing away obstacles, clearing away threats. All threats to that intelligence are cleared away. This is the style of protection here. Not allowing the intelligence to become obscured improves it. This is a different style of protection from the paranoid one of guarding against something, fending something off. The obscurations are removed, and that is the protection.

So mantra is the means or method. We have to have this skillful means in order to realize pain at the beginning. This is the hinayana approach to tantra, which is developing fundamental openness.

Pain is often very serious. Pain is often unspeakable. Not that it is difficult to describe, but we don't want to describe it. From that point of view, pain is synonymous with ego. Ego *is* pain, and pain *is* ego. Pain is neurosis.

Pain, or ego, is unspeakable. It's an enormous secret. It's such a big secret, we don't even have to name it. We can just barely make a reference to it and our colleague or friend will know what we're talking about. You might say, "Today's been a very heavy day." Your friend will never ask, "A heavy day of what?" It's understood. It's mystical communication.

Whenever the possibility of that kind of communication presents itself, we shy away from it. We go just so far and then we turn around. We don't go too far. Maybe we assume that if we went too far, it would be embarrassing for our colleague or friend. But actually it would be embarrassing to us (maybe to our friend or colleagues as well). Pain is the unnameable private parts we don't want to mention. It's a sacred name. It's a samsaric version of God. Its style of protection is the hesitation of not going into it as far as you can because you are threatened by the sense of going into it too far.

There is actually no danger in going too far. The danger, from ego's point of view, is that if we go too far, we may not know how to reassemble ourselves afterward. It's like the nursery rhyme about Humpty Dumpty: "All the king's horses and all the king's men couldn't put Humpty together again." There's no hope. Whatever power we can call on, the greatest of the greatest powers we can put together, cannot put our ego together again once it has been exposed. It is impossible, and we *know* that. We are so intelligent. There is a hint of tantra there already: we actually know how to protect ourselves from the protection of ego, that sense of an enormous scheme being there, even though it's a very simple little thing that is taking place. All that is the pain.

It is not so much the actual agony of having something like rheumatism or having been hurt psychologically by somebody and feeling bad about it. That is not quite the pain that is going on here. It is the fundamental mystical experience of "thisness," beingness, and unspeakableness—that thing we don't talk about to ourselves, let alone to others. We never even *think* of it. That is the pain. And there is a kind of intelligence there.

In Naropa's case, he wanted to overcome this pain, and he decided to leave his home and join a monastic establishment so he could expose himself to the mercies of the teachers and gurus—so he could give up, take refuge, give up arrogance, confusion, and so forth. But according to the example of Naropa's life, only exposing "this" is not quite enough.

Obviously in the West, with encounter groups, confession, psychiatrists, and so on, people have developed the idea of exposing the secret as far as you can, speaking your mind on religious, social, and philosophical subjects of all kinds. The methods range from taking part in orgies to becoming Cath-

olic and confessing oneself. There are so many ways of seemingly exposing oneself. We seem to have some understanding
about self-exposure, and we do our best. But that doesn't seem
to be quite the same thing we are doing here.

Not that I am criticizing every method that has been
developed so far in the West as a failure. Not at all. There is
an element of truth in all of them. We seem to be hitting the
right nail, but that doesn't mean that we are hitting it on the
head. We are hitting the general area of the nail anyway.
Generally, things are following the right pattern. Particularly,
spiritual, psychological, and philosophical developments that
have taken place in this country recently have been remarkably
intelligent. But the thing is: what happens then? Should we
keep repeating the same ceremonies of exposure of our ego
constantly, every day, every hour, every week? There is a limit
to how many times we can go to an orgy. There's a limit to
how many times we can go to confession. Repeating the same
thing over and over again at some point becomes a drug,
which gives a sense of relief, of openness or far-outness.

The problem here has nothing to do with the technique
being wrong. It is the attitude that seems to be wrong.
Through methods of exposing ourselves, we want to get rid of
the burden of this secret in us, because somebody might
recognize it and use it against us. That is usually the logic.
We want to get completely clear and clean so nobody can
attack us anymore.

That's a very smart scheme. But interestingly, sometimes
during the process of scheming we discover a new scheme. In
the process of going through the techniques and methods of
the first scheme, we find another method, another scheme.
We end up bombarded by all kinds of alternatives, and we are
never able to relate with any of them properly. We get
completely lost.

Or else we are very earnest and honest and follow one

method in a very methodical, businesslike fashion. We become professional orgy-goers, or professional encounter-groupies. In that way, we create another shell. The original trick doesn't work anymore. The trick of repeating the ceremony of uncovering ourselves creates another mask, a very thick mask, and once more we are embedded in the rock. Again and again it happens, and we can't get out of it. The methods themselves become obstacles. There is nothing we can do about it.

The problem seems to be the attitude that the pain should go, then we will be happy. That is our mistaken belief. The pain never goes, and we will never be happy. That is the truth of suffering, *duhkha satya*. Pain never goes; we will never be happy. There's a mantra for you. It's worth repeating. You've got the first initiation now: you've got a mantra.

It is not so much that pain is an obstacle. Rather, as we go on, pain becomes an obstacle because we want to get rid of it. Of course at the beginning we may not regard the pain as an obstacle. The first thing is stupidity: not realizing the pain. Then we realize the pain and we become familiar with the hang-ups connected with the pain. Then we want to get rid of that. That's the second veil, regarding the pain as an obstacle.

The idea is to learn to live with the pain in accordance with the Buddhist tradition of taking refuge. This is one of the very prominent, very important methods. Taking refuge here means surrendering hope rather than surrendering fear. When we give up promises, potentials, possibilities, then we begin to realize that there is no burden of further imprisonment. We have been completely freed, even from hope, which is a really refreshing experience. In other words, if we accept the burden as truly burdensome, completely burdensome, then its heaviness does not exist anymore. Because it is truly a burden, truly heavy. It is like identifying with a heavy rock that is pressing you into the ground. If you identify with the rock, you don't exist. You become the rock.

But that, too, becomes very tricky. Once you start looking at it that way, you can turn that into another trick. You create trick after trick that imprisons you with hope, until you finally realize there is no hope.

We are going to go through Naropa's life stage by stage and try to see how it applies to ourselves, rather than looking at it as the myth of Naropa, of a great teacher who got enlightened and lived happily ever after. There must be realities that connect his life with ours. This first step of hopelessness, for example, plays an extremely important part in realizing the foundations for tantra at the hinayana level of the Buddhist path. We can quite safely say that hope, or a sense of promise, is a hindrance on the spiritual path.

Creating this kind of hope is one of the most prominent features of spiritual materialism. There are all kinds of promises, all kinds of proofs. We find the same approach as that of a car salesman. Or it's like someone demonstrating a vacuum cleaner and telling you how well you could clean your house if you would just buy it. If you would just buy that vacuum cleaner, how beautiful your room would be, completely free of dirt and dust, down to the last speck! Whether it is a vacuum-cleaner salesman or a guru, we find the same level of salesmanship. That is why both are included in the same bag of materialists. There are so many promises involved. So much hope is planted in your heart. This is playing on your weakness. It creates further confusion with regard to pain. You forget about the pain altogether and get involved in looking for something other than the pain. And that itself *is* pain. Trying to suppress disbelief, focusing on belief, trying to convince yourself this approach will work (thinking that convincing yourself is what will make it work)—all that *is* pain.

That is what we will go through unless we understand that the basic requirement for treading the spiritual path is hopelessness. Hopelessness is not quite the same as despairing. There is a difference. Despair is laziness, lack of intellect. One is not even willing to look for the reason for the despair. It is a total flop. But hopelessness is very intelligent. You keep looking. You flip page after page, saying, "That's hopeless, that's hopeless." You are still very vigorous, hopelessly vigorous. You're still looking for hope, but each time you have to say, "Oh no. Yuck!" Hopelessness keeps going; it is very vigorous, very inspiring. It tickles your mind as though there were something you are about to discover. When you discover it, you say, "Ah, now I've found the thing! . . . Oh no. It's the same old thing again."

There is enormous challenge and excitement in hopelessness. When you give up, when you enter into complete despair with hopelessness after hopelessness, just before despair and laziness take you over, you begin to develop a sense of humor. You develop a sense of humor, and you don't become completely lazy and stupid.

STUDENT: In order for me to begin to attain hopelessness, I have to have some hope. It seems that I have to go back and forth between those two. It seems there has to be that pull from both sides.

TRUNGPA RINPOCHE: The first thing is not hope or a sense of promise as such; it's more like inquisitiveness, inquisitive mind, which explores constantly, including exploring yourself, your embarrassment about yourself, your insanity, your own confusion. That kind of inquisitiveness is not quite on the level of hope. But it is a definite step. Then, once you have found your hang-ups, your hesitation, then you begin to develop the project of getting rid of that pain and confusion.

That's what we always do anyway. There's no need for a program for that; that's just what we always do.

The minute you discover your hesitations, confusions, insanity, and so on, you want to get rid of them. You look for all kinds of remedies. You shop around and you find that fundamentally none of them work. They may work great temporarily, but fundamentally, they don't work. Then you start questioning. You question the products you bought at the supermarket. You look into each brand, the instructions on the label, and so on. The salespeople are very kind, making suggestions about the products. You go through all that, and you're still struggling. Then at a certain point it becomes necessary to let you have it: to tell you that the only and best remedy is hopelessness—which is your own product. It doesn't cost any money or energy. You don't have to go to the supermarket, and it's cheap and good. It's organic.

Many of you have already gone through this process. You have looked in the supermarket and seen the ads. You've seen it all. Now it's time to give up hope, even give up hope of attaining enlightenment.

STUDENT: Does despair come out of a relationship between energy and pain? If you were to fixate on pain, I think that would dissipate energy and bring despair.

TRUNGPA RINPOCHE: You see, energy is pain in some sense. But it is not one hundred percent. Maybe fifty-fifty. Energy and intelligence create pain. Intelligence in this case means ambition. You feel you have something to achieve that you're unable to achieve. You feel you might be unable to achieve your goal.

STUDENT: Sometimes I think I go looking for pain, that I cultivate it, and this seems masochistic. Also I think I see other people doing the same thing. What do you think of that?

TRUNGPA RINPOCHE: I think that sounds like a fascination or an occupation—trying to kill boredom. You don't want to look at the greater pain we're discussing—the unnameable. In order to avoid seeing that, you do anything to create a petty pain in order to avoid seeing the greater pain of "thisness," this "thing."

STUDENT: You said that the word *tantra* means "continuity," and that confuses me because my understanding is that one of the basic qualities of an enlightened person is the fact that he is not continuous, he is not solid at all. I thought that solidness was ego, and when he discovers that that's not real, then he's free to be not continuous.

TRUNGPA RINPOCHE: *Tantra* does mean "continuity." This kind of continuity cannot be challenged, because this kind of continuity never depends on superficial continuity or discontinuity. It is unconditional continuity. Obviously, the enlightenment experience involves the discontinuity of ego with its fixation, but there is also the element of all-pervasiveness—enlightenment is right now but later as well; we are enlightened now, but we will be more enlightened later. There is a thread of enlightenment that goes on all the time. The sense of the nonexistence of ego is the greatest continuity. So continuity here does not mean continuously relating to a single reference point. There is a state without reference point that is basic the way completely outer space, without stars and galaxies and planets, is basic. The stars, galaxies, and planets may be there or not, but still the space will be there.

S: And it contains everything.

TR: It contains nothing in this case, but still it contains itself. It does not need any feedback or maintenance—it does not need anything at all. That is the great umbrella above the little umbrellas.

STUDENT: Does the discovery of hopelessness take care of itself as you go through your life day by day, or is it something you have to work on? Do you have to go out of your way somehow?

TRUNGPA RINPOCHE: It's not easy. It wouldn't just dawn on you. You have to make a definite jump, which is a very painful one. Quite possibly you need another person to tell you you are hopeless. That is the role of a guru. You need a spiritual friend who says, "Now you're hopeless, and you will never be able to do anything. The outlook is full of nothingness." It seems to be the role of the guru to tell you that you are hopeless or that you will never solve your problem. It has to be a shock of some kind, otherwise it doesn't work. You would just continue on with your mild complaining of all kinds.

STUDENT: Rinpoche, would that shock of hopelessness create a sense of depression at that particular moment?

TRUNGPA RINPOCHE: Yes, I hope so.

STUDENT: I'm having a lot of trouble with your concept of pain. Pain to me is like feeling that I'm bleeding. And when I don't have that sense of pain, when I'm relieved of it, I say, "Well, I'm not in pain." My concept of pain is very visceral, and I feel it quite sharply. You're talking about a kind of pain that is still there when I'm relieved from my visceral pain and feeling good.

TRUNGPA RINPOCHE: I think you have a good understanding of what I mean. That's it. It's the larger notion, the whole thing: you're relieved of pain, and then what? There are a lot of loose ends. You try to look at everything officially as extending from one particular point to another particular point. You have certain boundaries that you don't go beyond. You can't be bothered. And beyond those boundaries are still greater loose ends. And those loose ends begin to lead back to you. Then you try to tidy them up again. This is the greater thing that we don't talk about that everybody knows about.

STUDENT: So these little pains are little things like having to find a job that can be tidied up temporarily.

TRUNGPA RINPOCHE: And that relates with the greater thing. But, you know, if you have an actual practical task to perform, you perform it.

S: But isn't being involved in performing that task some kind of hope? Do you have to give up performing the task?

TR: No, it's not as simple as that. You can go ahead and perform your task. But that doesn't solve your greater problem. Your problem is still there.

S: But you wouldn't even have to go through that to realize the larger situation.

TR: It depends on your intelligence. Some people dream too much, so they have to go through that. And some people already have a realistic vision of the prospects of their life, so they may not have to go through it.

STUDENT: You talked about the fact that we set up tricks for ourselves, getting involved with encounter groups and so on. We're tricking ourselves in some way in thinking that we're being more open and unmasking pain. What happens in hopelessness to those tricks? Does someone who's hopeless realize the tricks will never stop? That they will never end?

TRUNGPA RINPOCHE: I think so. That's good, yes.

STUDENT: Rinpoche, at the same time, I can't help but feel that there's a certain amount of joy attached to realizing the hopelessness of the situation. It seems that there's a sense of opposites coming together there.

TRUNGPA RINPOCHE: Yes, so what?

S: Well, it seems kind of incredible, this coming together of joy and pain.

TR: Well, that's the point. Hopelessness doesn't mean that you are miserable particularly. There's lots of room for energy, more energy and more joy. But *joy* is probably the wrong word—a sense of wholesomeness, healthiness, a sense of well-being because of hopelessness.

S: But somehow without ego.

TR: The sense of well-being does not have to have ego particularly.

S: Are we, evolutionarily speaking, on the verge of hopelessness? If you read the story of Naropa, it seems like Naropa went through so much.

TR: The level of hopelessness we are talking about came at the beginning of Naropa's life, before he became a pandit. We haven't had the level of his hopelessness in dealing with Tilopa yet. That's a tantric one. This is just the beginning level, which Naropa experienced when he took monk's vows and joined the monastery.

S: That sense of hopelessness that made him enter the monastery doesn't seem particularly hopeless. It sounds more like disillusionment. I mean, if you were talking to your parents about joining a dharma group and so on, you'd talk more about disillusionment with the mundane. . . .

TR: Yes, but once he entered the monastery, he began to feel that he was inadequate, and he started pushing too hard, speeding, and so forth. Hopelessness begins there.

S: Then he just wound up going out and looking for a guru.

TR: No. Then he found his intellect. He put himself together. He became a great pandit. Which probably we will talk about tomorrow.

S: So the hopelessness you're talking about is analogous to his hopelessness in the monastic situation.

TR: Yes. You see, things worked alternatingly. First intuition, then intellect, then intuition, and then the final level of intellect. So this was the first intuition—the desire to enter a monastery. Then he entered the monastery and found hopelessness. Then he found some way that clicked in which he could work with his intellect, some way in which his hopelessness became workable. This involved a big chunk of intellect—studying the Tripitaka to the point of knowing it inside out, and so on. Then he came back to the level of intuition again when he began to look for Tilopa. And finally, when he was completely absorbed in Tilopa's teaching and had become enlightened, then he went back to intellect again. At that point, instead of being *prajna*, intellect became *jnana*, wisdom.

STUDENT: Between intellect and intuition, is one more valid than the other?

TRUNGPA RINPOCHE: Both of them are valid, just like your head and arms.

S: What's the difference between them?

TR: Intellect has nothing to do with book learning, becoming a scholar, particularly. It is analytical mind, which is able to see things clearly and precisely. And intuition feels things on the level of pain and pleasure.

2

Giving Birth to Intellect

WE HAVE DISCUSSED Naropa's first discovery of pain, or our own discovery of the meaning of Naropa's example, our own discovery of pain. This is a kind of adolescent level, involved with the discovery of the world and its meanings. Naropa joins a monastery—or you join a meditation center. He becomes part of a *vihara,* which is parallel with becoming part of our meditation center here.

Then, very interestingly, in the midst of practice, suddenly aggression arises—enormous anger and resentment. One does not recognize where this aggression comes from. One does not even want to trace it back. But this aggression arises. There is the aggression of having been tricked into becoming part of an established, disciplined setup, the aggression that says things should happen properly but they are not functioning the way you expected. The sense of aggression becomes everything. In fact there is enormous awareness; an almost meditative level of absorption in aggression and resentment takes place. You are resentful that your instructor has been unreasonable to you, has disciplined you unreasonably, blamed something on you that you didn't do. There is a certain sense of disgust. In the middle of practice there are occasional thoughts of quitting and leaving the place, and you daydream about how to work out the project of leaving in detail. But there is also some hesitation; or the project becomes so big that you are afraid to embark on it.

All this kind of aggression takes place after you begin to realize pain, the truth of pain, as a definite thing that you cannot ignore, that you cannot forget. This pain is real pain. You experience this not because you trust and believe doctrines you have been told. Rather your real pain has become obvious. It is not somebody's doctrine. You have discovered your own truth of pain.

This creates a sense of imprisonment, because what you've discovered coincides with what is taught in the books. Being imprisoned in this way by your own realization of pain is by no means pleasant. At the same time, it is exciting that in fact you are in immediate and direct communication with the truth. There is some sense of promise, but not a sense of a happy ending.

The more you look into this situation, the more horrific it becomes. That is the course that the aggression takes. You are resentful about something—about the world, the books, the people, the environment, the lifestyle—and at the same time you resent your own existence, because you are the creator of the pain and you can't escape from yourself. The more you think about it, the more the whole thing becomes grimmer and grimmer and grimmer. Trying to reach out and kick the nearest piece of furniture doesn't help. Being rude to your colleagues doesn't help. Somehow, complaining about the food doesn't help either. An inevitable depression, a mystical depression, a very powerful one, comes with anger and resentment.

You might ask if this is good or bad. We can't say that it's good or that it's bad. But it *is*. It certainly does exist.

All that anger and resentment and pain, depression, sexual frustration, financial frustration—the things of all kinds that go on in one's head—have one good thing about them. There is one good message here, a really good one, a gem that we are about to discover in ourselves. It is not good in the sense of relieving pain and bringing happiness. It's another subtle form of pain, but it contains an enormous jewel, enormous richness, enormous beauty. It is called intellect. This pain that is happening in you and around you, that is trying to give birth and is not able to, is a message that intellect is just about to be born.

In Naropa's case, he was locked up in a monastic cell. Traditionally, you have an eight-by-eight room. You have to rise at four in the morning and go to sleep about midnight. In the courtyard of the monastery at night, a monk who keeps discipline with his big stick keeps walking around checking to make sure that everybody is up and studying, memorizing scriptures. You read by the dim light of an oil lamp. You read the scriptures, memorize them, and meditate on them.

In the monastery, the only relief comes when you change subjects of study or switch meditative techniques. You meditate and the gong goes; the only break you have is going to study. Then you study and the gong goes, and your only relief is to go back to meditation. Eating in the assembly hall is not particularly festive either. It's as though you are on trial. The monk in charge of discipline might come and reprimand you for your lack of mindfulness at any time. You're not allowed to jump or run. You walk mindfully and you speak softly. You're not allowed to shout. You're not even allowed to draw doodles.

Life at Nalanda University was very dignified, fundamentally very sane, but at the same time very severe. According to historical records, the architecture there was good, wonderful, but it was designed to suit monks. It was not at all lavish or luxurious. The basic minimum was provided. The monks had the encouragement of simplicity and awareness. The walls were designed to bounce back one's own neurotic thoughts. Every inch of one's life was planned, and particular behavior was prescribed for all situations.

The resentment that one can develop in such situations brings prajna. Great teachers like Naropa and Atisha Dipankara and Saraha—a lot of great teachers of that age—came out of such establishments. The resentment turns into prajna. Prajna is a Sanskrit word. *Jna* means "knowledge," and *pra* means "supreme." So prajna is supreme knowledge or greater knowledge.

We mustn't confuse that with wisdom. In the nontheistic tradition of Buddhism, knowledge comes first and wisdom comes later. Wisdom is connected with looking, and knowledge is connected with seeing. Knowledge is seeing, being aware. We have to learn how to see first. Having learned how to see, then we begin to look, which is on the wisdom level, the ultimate level.

Prajna is seeing things as they are. At the beginning, if you look without the training of seeing, you don't look at things as they are, because you don't see them. Seeing here is a matter of both awareness and discipline. You're aware of this room. You're aware of the temperature in this room, and you're aware of sitting on chairs. You have a general kind of awareness of how and where you are. The way intellect goes with that is: within a state of being, such as being here and sitting on chairs, you can function. You can sit there and at the same time you can think and write and look. This manifestation of one's state of being is intellect.

So the intellect we are talking about is not the bookworm type. It doesn't necessarily mean being a scholar or doing research work or anything like that. Intellect in the sense of prajna is a state of being logical and open, open to any information and willing to collect it, chew it, swallow it, digest it, work with it. This is not the ordinary idea of intellect connected with intellectuals in intellectual circles. There you are given a certain reference point. You are already programmed before you know who and what you are. You are given certain raw material, and you have to fit that raw material into certain pigeonholes that are already prepared for you.

In the case of prajna, you have the raw material with you, but you don't have the pigeonholes. If you like, you can build a pigeonhole for yourself. In that sense, with prajna everything is homemade; that is why it is greater intellect. The only system you have is that of sharpening your intellect working within the relative frame of reference of logic. Let's take the example of saying, "I feel sick." The reason why I feel sick is that I have the memory "I used to be well; I used to feel fine." I know that I am sick because, compared with that memory, I don't feel good. It's very simple, ordinary logic like that.

Prajna is also the seed of discriminating awareness. In discriminating awareness, you take things in openly, accept everything, but at the same time everything is examined critically. Being critical in this sense is not rejecting and accepting things in a petty way. It is seeing the values of each thing in its own place, rather than seeing its values from the point of view of whether it is threatening to your ego or helpful to it. You see things as they are with dispassionate judgment. This is again the quality of prajna, greater knowledge or transcendent knowledge—seeing dispassionately but still discriminating.

This is very painful in a way. When you begin to see things without any value judgment in the ordinary sense, without any bias regarding yourself and others, your vision and your logic and your sharpness become very painful. You don't have any filters between you and "that"; you are touching a cold stone. Reality becomes a pain in the ass. An analogy that has been used for that kind of seeing is: on a winter morning, licking a rock with frost on it; your tongue sticks to the rock because your tongue is very naked and warm and the stone is so cold. You think you are licking it, but actually your tongue is stuck. That is reality as seen with prajna. It is so immediate, and it sticks there. That's the kind of pain we are talking about.

The prajna level of pain is so immediate and so, so powerful. The level of pain we were discussing before is relatively mild—in fact, in many ways luxurious. Pain on the prajna level is much more painful than that earlier pain, because before we didn't have a chance to apply our intellect to it. We just felt painful, were imprisoned in the pain. Of course there was some kind of intellect functioning, but not one hundred percent the way it is on the prajna level. Now we are relating with naked reality without any dualistic padding.

The notion of duality here is not that there are separate things existing and therefore we can speak of duality. The notion of duality here is that things are one, and a big barrier has been put in the middle, which divides it. The oneness on the other side is called "that," and the oneness on this side is called "this." Because of the Suez Canal we built, because of the wall we built, the one is slashed in two. And nonduality is not a matter of the two things melting back into each other, but of taking that barrier completely out. When that happens and the two aspects of the one meet, we find it is quite painful, because we are so used to having separate entities there. Now when we realize that nonduality is being imposed on us, we find it very claustrophobic, very sharp. It is much too sharp and much too powerful to meet this oneness. The "that" does not adjust to the "this," and the "this" does not adjust to the "that." Once the barrier is removed, they become one with no chance for adjustment at all. That's why the prajna experience is so sharp and immediate and powerful—highly powerful, extraordinarily powerful.

At this prajna level, pain is seen as a hundred times bigger than we saw it at the beginning. You have acquired a brand-new, very powerful microscope, and your little pain is put under that microscope, and you look at it. You see a gigantic monster. And that's not even at the level of tantra yet. We are just barely beginning. But you cannot say that seeing the pain in this magnified way is an exaggeration at all. It is seeing things as they are in their own right perspective, seeing clearly by putting a small object under the microscope.

Naropa began to enjoy being in his monastic cell, being watched and being worked hard, because he was learning how to use language, how to communicate, how to think logically, how to work logically. He engaged in debates; he practiced and he studied, memorized texts. And he felt very comfortable. But at the same time, he felt tortured by his rediscovery of reality from the mahayana point of view. As far as we are concerned, we have a lot to learn from the example of his life. We could learn to trust in our intellect.

I suppose we should make a distinction between analytical mind and intellectual mind. In the case of analytical mind, you already have formulas that have been given to you, and you try to use those formulas to analyze things you come across. You interpret in accordance with certain given methods. With intellectual mind free from analytical mind, the only formula you have is basic logic—you are without set ideas and patterns; you are not bound by any social, philosophical, or religious standards. You are free from that indoctrination; therefore you are able to see your pain more magnified, as though under a microscope. That is the main difference between analytical mind and intellectual mind, intellectual mind being synonymous with prajna.

Another thing about analytical mind is that there is a certain amount of aggression involved in it. You are defending your faith. You are analyzing in such a way as to fit something into an already worked out reference point, and there is a spare part missing. Therefore you are studying matters concerning that spare part. Then, having discovered the spare part, you have to make it fit into the original body—which is very aggressive and very demanding, and it makes you totally blind. You fail to see the rest of the whole. Whereas intellect in the sense of prajna is very open and has never been given a particular project. The only project there is for prajna is to see totality and clarity. In order to understand the parts, you have to relate with the whole body rather than concentrating on the parts. That seems to be prajna's style.

STUDENT: Where does the emotional element come in with prajna? If pain is magnified a hundred times, a lot of emotions must come along with that. Does prajna have the ability to handle those emotions?

TRUNGPA RINPOCHE: We don't have that ability at this point. We don't have the equipment to deal with emotions yet—that is, Naropa doesn't yet have it. That was why he was led on to tantra. He realized that, instead of everything being so clear-cut, he had another problem. The level of prajna we've talked about so far has nothing to do with emotions as such. It's just intellect. It's like the level of a teenager in the puberty stage who is still fascinated by gadgets, who is never concerned with affects and emotions—anger or aggression or anything like that. He is just rediscovering the universe constantly.

S: With logic leading.

TR: Yes, that's precisely how Naropa was.

STUDENT: I thought it was one of the failings of analytical mind that it doesn't take into account the rawer aspects of experiences but rather deals in abstractions. I don't see how prajna or what you call intellectual mind can operate without relating to the emotions.

TRUNGPA RINPOCHE: Analytical mind can analyze the emotions, but there are still certain dogmas and philosophical ideas involved. Prajna, or the intellect, sees emotions as loose ends; it sees them very technically—as part of the five *skandhas,* for example. From the point of view of prajna, you don't have to get into them particularly. You see them clearly and in fact could describe them to other people and help them. But still this doesn't really work when compared to the tantric level. It doesn't become as fully emotional as it should be, could be. In prajna, you can relate to the raw material by having confidence. You don't really have to get into it exactly. You have to relate to it personally, but not on the emotional level as such.

STUDENT: Is the intellectual approach what the arhats over-stressed?

TRUNGPA RINPOCHE: The arhats didn't seem to do that very much. It seems to have been the young ambitious pandits like Naropa, people newly converted to prajna with its dispassionate kind of clarity. Those are the bodhisattvas up to the seventh *bhumi.*

STUDENT: How is it possible to work through the confusions of the lower bhumis and still maintain that kind of distance?

TRUNGPA RINPOCHE: You can, because your mind is so sharp. Your mind is extraordinarily sharp, and there are no obstacles to it at all. It can see through anything right away. But that is not the same as involving yourself in the confusion or emotion fully, being completely in it, which could happen.

I think the problem on the prajna level is that relationships are taken as a basic reference point with regard to each other, and emotions are taken as a basic reference point with regard to each other. The only thing lacking here is the highest form of fundamental rawness and ruggedness found on the tantric level. Although there is only a superficial understanding of the raw material, there is a certain amount of fearlessness at the same time. You do not hesitate to deal with things as they are, but you are still at the level of seeing. That fearlessness is possible if your mind is really tuned into prajna, the sword of Manjushri. The sword of Manjushri cuts constantly; it never stays in its sheath.

STUDENT: Is it prajna the way we see and hear everything happening without having any power to stop it or pick and choose? Then subsequently we sort it all out; a split second later we pick and choose. Is prajna the primary receptivity before we say things like, "I like tall more than short?"

TRUNGPA RINPOCHE: Yes, I think so.

S: If you could live totally in that, without the second judgment, without the subsequent activity of the mind, would there be a familiarity from when you knew both things?

TR: Both things?

S: Yes. First you see something clearly, without the overlay quality of judgment. But then, as you go on judging what you saw, you familiarize yourself with it more or less. But before that familiarization, before your bias becomes involved, is there still a sense of familiarity with what you see, or does it become something strange?

TR: I think there's still familiarity, because there's trust in one's own intellect. You may be dealing with completely alien raw material, but at the same time there's trust in your own intelligence, which creates another level of familiarity with things. It's like a confident general conducting warfare on the battlefield. He probably doesn't know the nature of his enemy, but he's confident he can wipe him out.

STUDENT: Rinpoche, what is aware of prajna? Prajna being

awareness of various things, is there something that is aware of prajna? Or is prajna aware of prajna?

TRUNGPA RINPOCHE: There are two levels to that. The first level is prajna being aware of itself in such a way that it cuts its own blade. It's so fast and so precise that it cuts itself. This doesn't blunt its blade; that blade sharpens itself by cutting itself. Then there is another level, which is the awareness of skillful means. It is aware of how and when to use the sword. The use of the sword creates feedback to the swordsman.

But prajna is by no means regarded as absolute. It is still a relative experience, because striking with a sword is going from here to there. Even though the sword may have two edges, while you're cutting "that," you can't cut "this." You have to cut "this" after "that" has been cut. So there is still a process and a journey involved, which brings a sense of skill, a sense of confidence. The blade of the sword is accuracy and wakefulness, and the body of the sword is confidence and delight in itself.

S: Is prajna cutting itself similar to disowning your own insight?

TR: Definitely, yes. Prajna is an ongoing process—constantly cutting, all the time. So all the time it is cutting, it has to sharpen its own blade. Otherwise you would have to stop cutting to sharpen the blade. So it's an inbuilt mechanism, so to speak. Cutting through sharpens itself, because it cuts itself as soon as it cuts the other.

STUDENT: Is this sense of confidence the reason that prajna can't handle emotions?

TRUNGPA RINPOCHE: Well, we can't really say that prajna can't handle emotions; rather, emotions never occur on the prajna level; emotions are no longer a part of that particular level. They are just irrelevant from that point of view. Emotions are not particularly dealt with, and the problem of emotions never occurred.

S: Because prajna is just seeing?

TR: Yes.

STUDENT: I was wondering a bit more about the relationship between resentment and prajna. Did you mean to say that resentment caused prajna? Or when that kind of resentment comes on, it's already prajna, understanding?

TRUNGPA RINPOCHE: The resentment gives birth to prajna. You give birth to a sword. It begins to cut through your insides, and there is all kinds of pain and resentment, and you don't know who to blame. Then suddenly, unexpectedly, you give birth to a sword.

S: You described the situation at Nalanda as a typical highly disciplined monastic situation and gave the impression that just the very irritation of the situation contributes toward the development of prajna.

TR: Yes.

S: How does that work? Can irritation cause intellect?

TR: Irritations are intellect, you could quite safely say. Irritations come from logical mind of some kind or other. Without that, we couldn't be irritated.

S: Then I could give a person a little gift of prajna by putting a pebble in his shoe?

TR: Sure. That sharpens prajna.

S: Is that one of the reasons behind a very tight and claustrophobic meditation schedule?

TR: Anything. Anything. Yes, anything.

S: You mean yes and more?

TR: Yes and more, yes. Since we can't have eight-by-eight meditation cells for everybody, we can create time cells.

STUDENT: You said that at the prajna level, emotions are not seen as a problem, and apparently it can go on like that. I still don't understand that.

TRUNGPA RINPOCHE: At the level of prajna, emotions don't apply as a problem, because prajna is very much speeding along, constantly speeding. In order for emotions to ferment, you have to wait for a little while. That explains the analogy of Naropa sitting reading a book. He is obviously constantly cutting through, but here he has relatively slowed down, slowed down a little bit. He has decided to relax a little bit, and for lack of something better to do, to read a book. And then the message came to him that we will be discussing soon.

STUDENT: It seems that a little while ago you were implying that the way to give birth to prajna is by increasing the level of irritation as much as possible. It seems that it really couldn't be that simple, or we could really go wild irritating each other and help each other give birth to prajna.

TRUNGPA RINPOCHE: It's not as simple as that, that's true. I wasn't really recommending putting things in people's shoes as a practical approach. In fact, that level of irritation can be created just by giving a little space to people. In that way the equivalent of Naropa's setup can be created in a Vermont farmhouse. We are not as learned as Naropa and his colleagues. We don't have such a lavish property. We don't have the patronage of the kings. But still we can do a pretty good job.

STUDENT: Does prajna have a sense of compassion?

TRUNGPA RINPOCHE: It has a sense of trust in oneself,

which is basic compassion, warmth, toward oneself. That automatically happens. Without that, you wouldn't be holding a sword. You wouldn't strike because you'd mistrust yourself. The reason the sword of prajna can be handled by a person is that he has a certain amount of trust in himself.

STUDENT: Is prajna related to what Don Juan calls clarity?[1]

TRUNGPA RINPOCHE: We can't discuss the Don Juan issue at the level of prajna. Basically, it is at the level of tantra. There is that element of clarity, which is a hint of prajna at a higher, more mystical level, higher than the mahayana level we are discussing. Obviously, tantra does have prajna.

S: Don Juan says that when clarity develops, it becomes your enemy.

TR: That has something to do with energy. You see, on the prajna level, there is not very much relating to energy as such. Sharpness is the only energy. The other energy I am referring to is a kind of fertility, energy that gives birth to itself. That doesn't happen on the mahayana level; it only happens in tantra.

STUDENT: Do you have to cut everything down before the fertility begins to happen?

TRUNGPA RINPOCHE: I think so, yes. It's more of a plowing process, actually. You have to plow twice. Once to tame the ground and then again to sow the seed.

STUDENT: Does the difference between prajna and jnana, knowledge and wisdom, seeing and looking, have to do with the birth of some kind of aim in a person? Your sword just functions, cuts anything that comes into view. But wisdom would be not having to do that—knowing what you're after and therefore knowing when to cut and when not to.

TRUNGPA RINPOCHE: Prajna is discovering the weapon and the technique for using it. But there is no master there to conduct the whole scheme. Jnana is discovering the wise schemer. At that level you have the plan that is not planned deliberately, and you also have the weapon and the swordsman. At that point it becomes a complete kingdom. That's why the buddhas are sometimes referred to in the scriptures as kings or victorious ones. Bodhisattvas are called princes—they're still on the adolescent level.

This contrasts with the look-and-see approach, which is connected with an external deity or God. You have to put an effort into perceiving an external being who is greater. But in the case of the nontheistic tradition, there is no reference to an outsider. There is rediscovering within. That results in the difference between looking in order to see and seeing in order to look.

STUDENT: You were talking about trust in oneself. It seems to me that could only be real after prajna is born. Up until that point, how can you distinguish between ego-based self-confidence and trust in oneself?

TRUNGPA RINPOCHE: Ego doesn't cut its own ground. Ego nurses its ground. An egoless experience like prajna cuts its own ground. That's where the irritations and resentment we have been talking about come from. And within the realm of resentment, a soft heart begins to develop, softness toward oneself. The softer you become toward yourself, the more you want to cut your ground. Somehow the question of ego doesn't apply at that point. Ego is already dissipating and has given up its hold on you. This is an organic thing that happens slowly. Somebody might ask you later, "What happened to your ego?" And you might say, "Oh, I never thought about that."

STUDENT: Resentment gives way to being soft to yourself, and the more soft toward yourself you are, the more you have a need to cut away your own ground? I don't quite follow.

TRUNGPA RINPOCHE: Softness here is a sense of being kind to yourself.

S: How does that grow from resentment?

TR: It grows from resentment because resentment is very intelligent; anger is very intelligent; depression is very intelligent. And usually you are angry at yourself because subconsciously you wanted to be kind to yourself. Otherwise you wouldn't get angry. If you weren't wanting to be kind to yourself, you might just as well give in, let yourself be destroyed. The resentment is an outward-directed defense mechanism for protecting yourself, which automatically suggests a sense of softness, a soft spot in oneself.

S: So where does the cutting come in, the desire to cut more the more one feels the soft spot?

TR: Well, one doesn't cut oneself; one cuts one's ground, which is the same thing resentment does, actually. This is completely the opposite of ego. The ordinary ego approach is that you hate yourself and you love your ground. You are constantly building up your ground, your territory. Still you regard yourself with distaste. It is suicidal. It's the reverse psychology of what develops when people are put into a monastic situation and disciplined in the way we talked about. They begin to change their logic. They begin to resent the environment rather than themselves. They reject the ground and want to preserve themselves—which is compassion.

STUDENT: Does the resentment come from seeing through the veil that covers the pain?

TRUNGPA RINPOCHE: Yes.

S: And does that high degree of irritation bring a high degree of awareness at the same time, because you're right there?

TR: Yes, yes.

S: So the resentment is actually intelligence itself.

TR: You can't have resentment without being intelligent.

STUDENT: Is resentment an emotion?

TRUNGPA RINPOCHE: There is a definite technical problem with that. Emotion is supposed to be a fundamental, organic process. Resentment may be the vanguard of the emotions, but it is not a real emotion, because it relates with the fringe, the edge of things. Resentment is edgy and not quite hearty.

S: What are real emotions?

TR: Different expressions of being and different ways of relating with being. For example, if you feel your being is lacking something, you create passion. If you feel your being is threatened, you create aggression—and so on. It's connected with a total sense of being. The total sense of being feels not quite complete enough, and you try to balance that. Real emotions are much more dignified than things like resentment, which are at the level of the outskirts. The emotions are the real capital rather than the profit.

STUDENT: Rinpoche, can resentment give way to real emotion if you are willing to get into it?

TRUNGPA RINPOCHE: It could. You see, the resentment we are talking about here is a very special kind of resentment—spiritual-journey resentment. Ordinary resentment doesn't develop; it just goes back and forth, because there's no journey. There's no heart. There's no particular pattern. It's just random.

STUDENT: Would you say an emotion like anger is an

expression of your pain, or isn't it rather ego's attempt to cover up the pain—in a sense, to escape itself?

TRUNGPA RINPOCHE: Sure. I think so. Basically the shyness of ego doesn't want to face itself, so it tends to bring up all kinds of things.

STUDENT: If you feel very angry, then there seems to be a need to get beyond your anger.

TRUNGPA RINPOCHE: That depends on the student's level. At the beginner's level, anger has never been understood or experienced properly. Anger has to be acknowledged. At the more advanced level, I suppose we could say that anger can be transmuted into a working basis.

STUDENT: Does that require trust in your anger? Or trust in yourself?

TRUNGPA RINPOCHE: Those two amount to the same thing. Yes, something like that. There is an all-pervasive trust happening in that area. Usually the problem comes when you and your anger are in conflict. The problem is being in conflict with your emotions, which makes things very uncomfortable. If you had no conflict with your emotions, things would be very natural. If there is no conflict, that solves seventy-five percent of the problem.

S: What's the other twenty-five percent?

TR: Self-consciousness about having solved your problem.

S: What do you do about that?

TR: You don't do anything about that. It just falls apart.

3

Choiceless Awareness

PRAJNA SEEMS TO be a way of opening many gates. Through prajna one discovers the real meaning of *shunyata*. Discovering shunyata is very powerful, and it is also frightening. Prajna could be described as a way of opening up the shunyata experience—that is, a way of being cornered. You get cornered into "this" to the extent that finally you have to escape through the walls. That is, you have to see the walls as empty; otherwise, you cannot escape.

Shunyata is more of a meditative experience than intellect is. It is often referred to as choiceless awareness—you do not develop an understanding of shunyata, but rather it comes to you. When a person has developed his intellect—clarity and sharpness—to a certain level, that provides a kind of ground that makes it possible for him to see the nonexistence of shunyata—and the fullness of shunyata at the same time.

You might say, "But what's left after prajna has done its cutting through?" There is lots left. The process of cutting through also has to be exposed, to the point where the journey no longer exists, the process doesn't exist anymore, the effort doesn't exist anymore. Shunyata is truly choiceless and does not compromise. Once you realize that you have no ground at all, none whatsoever, you are suspended in midair. When you cry for help, nobody is around you, and your voice itself becomes shunyata, so you can't even shout. Your actions to save yourself become nonexistent, which is the result of cutting through. Because you have cut through so much, finally your own ground has been cut through completely. Then the process of cutting through no longer exists. There is no occupation of any kind at all.

We should understand as a general principle the logic of subject and object and their duality, which I mentioned in the previous talk. Duality is not composed of two separate entities. Subject and object are not two different entities. They are one. By creating a wall within the one, we produce duality. Thus shunyata is simply an expansion of "this." That is why it is called choiceless awareness. "This" pushes the walls out; "this" expands.

You might ask, "If only 'this' exists, does that conflict with the general idea of egolessness?" Absolutely not. Ego and egolessness have nothing to do with "this." Actually ego is based on "that"; failing to realize "this" is what created ego. So the more you realize "this" or "here," the more groundless you become.

You don't have to have ground, but as I mentioned already, at the beginning this is rather frightening. There is an analogous moment in Naropa's life. He had been training for eight years in the monastery and had passed his oral examination, which took the form of logical debates, and he had become the head of Nalanda. At that point he had a vision of an ugly woman, which was a shock, a sudden shock. According to traditional interpretations, this woman was Vajrayogini, who is a symbol of shunyata. The sudden shock of shunyata was overwhelming. Her shadow fell on the book he was reading—this was the terrifying experience of shunyata. After being through lots and lots of cutting through, so much prajna, you finally realize you have no choice but to seek the guru. This is the result of prajna, intellect. But at the same time you might say that shunyata itself is also a form of intellect, the highest form. The ugly woman's intellect was much sharper and more powerful than Naropa's was at the time. But at the level of shunyata, intellect is really no longer regarded as prajna. At that level there is an awareness that is an expression of further compassion. The aspect of softness or nonaggression becomes very intelligent, but not intellectual, not sharp in the style of prajna in action. It is sharp in the manner of prajna as a state of being, so to speak.

Of course things don't happen as linearly as that. We could have an experience of prajna and a glimpse of shunyata happening simultaneously within ourselves. We could have that. We cut our ground and have a frightening—terrifying— sudden glimpse of groundlessness. Then we try to latch back onto our ground. This sort of thing happens constantly to us if we have any awareness of a journey taking place on the spiritual path. You might make the pretense or actually think that you are freaking out, losing your grip on reality, but it is a mere glimpse of shunyata taking place.

Shunyata is also described in terms of the feminine principle—as the consort of all the buddhas. Prajna is described in terms of the feminine principle too—as the mother of all the buddhas, she who gives birth to the very idea of enlightenment. This very notion was started by her, by prajna. But she who made the buddhas speak, communicate, is shunyata. Because with shunyata there is a lot of room, openness, groundlessness, therefore there is no fear of communicating with students as Buddha communicated with his disciples. In the situation of groundlessness, no one is standing on any ground, so communication can take place quite freely.

In Naropa's song after he meets the ugly woman [pp. 25– 26 in Guenther's translation], each line is connected with a different attribute of samsara. It shows that somehow his sense of imprisonment has been sharpened. He realizes his inadequacy in being unable to see the reality of shunyata. He has enough prajna, but that doesn't help him anymore. He remains in a state of limbo. Prajna without shunyata is a body without arms, as is traditionally said, like a body without arms trying to climb a rock.

I suppose in order to simplify matters, we could say the real definition of shunyata is awareness without choice, or awareness that contains no experience. That is why shunyata is described as full and empty at the same time. Emptiness here does not mean seeing everything as just energy, so that you could walk through tables and chairs. Rather you begin to see yourself as tables and chairs or rocks and sky and water. You begin to identify with the phenomenal world completely. Your existence is one of those phenomena, so everything is transparent or fluid. There is a sense of uniformity, sameness. At the same time there is a sense of difference.

STUDENT: Is shunyata like mindfulness in that you identify with phenomena?

TRUNGPA RINPOCHE: No, I wouldn't say its like mindfulness practice. In the usual approach to mindfulness practice, you project onto "that," onto the tables and chairs. You are the instigator. In the case of shunyata, to a certain extent, the tables and chairs become the instigator. They become the reminder.

S: I thought mindfulness was just seeing things as they are, observing but not reflecting. So in that sense I thought mindfulness and shunyata would be the same.

TR: Yes, in that sense, but it's rather tricky. You see, mindfulness contains the idea that you are the original instigator. You thought of the idea of mindfulness, rather than having a sense of becoming one of the phenomena. Shunyata is all-pervasive; awareness becomes ubiquitous.

STUDENT: What did you mean when you said that in shunyata there's awareness but no experience?

TRUNGPA RINPOCHE: Experience is a process like eating food. You pick it up, you put it in your mouth, you chew it, and you swallow it. Experience is a process like that if we look at it in slow motion. It may happen very fast, but if we look at it in slow motion, it contains those steps. The content of the experience has to be adapted to one's own being. In this case, no adaptation is needed. It's a one-shot deal, so to speak.

STUDENT: You describe shunyata in terms of nonduality and everything becoming "this," and you talk about pushing out the walls of "this." That all sounds as though there is some maintenance involved, which doesn't really fit.

TRUNGPA RINPOCHE: I suppose it is the opposite of maintenance. Pushing out the walls is a kind of transcendental vandalism.

S: Still there's the idea of the wall being pushed out. And what's on the other side of the wall?

TR: Nothing. Just the other side.

S: Is that a painful experience?

TR: It's shocking.

STUDENT: Presumably it's not self-conscious enough to be exactly painful.

TRUNGPA RINPOCHE: Yes, it's not exactly painful. Pain is conditional on one's maintaining oneself, and this is just an experience of expanding "this," so there's a certain amount of confidence in the needlessness of maintaining oneself. So it's a surprise. There is a sense of the needlessness of maintaining oneself, but still there is an ongoing process of naiveté. This experience cuts through the naiveté, and suddenly you're seeing something extraordinary arising out of a very ordinary thing. When one is naive, one expects things to stay as they are; one doesn't expect any surprises. The shunyata experience cuts through that naiveté.

STUDENT: You said that prajna's cutting through to shunyata didn't involve pain. But didn't the visions that Naropa had when he was looking for Tilopa express different aspects of his pain?

TRUNGPA RINPOCHE: We are talking about a different level. We haven't got to that level yet. That's something much more subtle and also much more painful. This is just sort of a rehabilitation process that's taking place now.

S: Well, didn't he find it rather painful when the woman implied he didn't understand the sense of what he was reading?

TR: Not really. If Naropa were to have experienced pain at that point, it would have been because he resented his greatness as a pandit being undermined and insulted. But somehow his state of mind was so sharp that there wasn't any room for that. He took in the message immediately, very clearly, very simply. That's because of the sharpness of prajna. If he had had the slightest involvement with spiritual materialism, he would have been very hurt. But since he didn't, the whole thing was very clear.

STUDENT: If, in the shunyata experience, there's no ground, no subconscious thing going on, does that mean that everything feels extremely fresh and new?

TRUNGPA RINPOCHE: I would say that the first experience would feel new because you haven't had it before. You're still wearing out your hang-ups, so it seems to be new. But once you've become an adult in shunyata, a professional with it, so to speak, instead of seeing things as new, you see them as very ordinary and full of details. Ordinary things full of details. It might feel fresh, not on account of its newness, but rather on account of its ordinariness.

S: Then there's nothing exciting about it.

TR: The details are very exciting, constantly. And there is a potential of mahamudra in seeing the details in their fullness, in their energy aspect. The emptiness is the meditative aspect.

STUDENT: If, in shunyata, there's no process and no experiencer, what's the relationship to the teachings? Ordinarily we would relate to the teachings as a reference point in a process, and it seems that in shunyata that too would dissolve.

TRUNGPA RINPOCHE: You see, this is precisely the point where the teachings become part of you. You are completely identified with the teachings. You yourself become a living teaching; you yourself become living dharma. That's the way it is from this point on up to the highest level of vajrayana. There is constant identification with the teaching. It becomes more and more part of your body, part of your brain, part of your heart. The more you identify with the teachings, the more the reference point takes the form of awareness that constantly reminds you. That's why shunyata is called choiceless awareness. Because you have identified with the teachings, awareness comes to you.

STUDENT: You often speak of aloneness and of the spiritual path as a lonely journey. It sounds like shunyata is the first real experience of aloneness.

TRUNGPA RINPOCHE: Very much so. Yes, there's no ground. But it feels very tough at the same time. We have an expression—"hard fact"—that seems to fit.

STUDENT: Does discipline become more relaxed at this point, more self-initiating?

TRUNGPA RINPOCHE: Very much so. The idea is that when you become more identified with the teachings, discipline becomes a natural habit. On the level of shunyata, discipline becomes very organic, ordinary, spontaneous.

STUDENT: Is the *satori* experience of Zen an experience of shunyata?

TRUNGPA RINPOCHE: Yes. I think the peak of the shunyata experience is what satori is. The peak of shunyata, a real glimpse of shunyata. Your logic wears out. You have no logic, no reference point of logic, and you become completely exposed to nothingness, or fullness. That is the satori experience of a sudden glimpse of aloneness.

STUDENT: That seems to have a very different taste from Naropa's meeting with the old woman.

TRUNGPA RINPOCHE: Not so different, actually. The only difference is that there are tantric overtones in the images in his life, like meeting the old woman. In the Zen tradition, you don't have a dialogue with Zen. You might have a dialogue with a buddha or somebody else. Nobody has a dialogue with Zen. But here, Naropa is having a dialogue with Zen. That's just a tantric way of looking at the situation.

STUDENT: Is there some reason Naropa doesn't look for a teacher until he's had the experience of shunyata?

TRUNGPA RINPOCHE: He never thought of a teacher from that angle. Obviously he did have a lot of masters, professors, and so forth—teachers but not gurus. The idea of a guru never occurred to him before. He was satisfied that he was being taught, that he was learning, that he was a good student. He never thought in terms of a real teacher who could lead him beyond the technical, theoretical, prajna level.

STUDENT: When the old woman told him he understood the words but not the sense, it seems to me that would be a criticism of analytical mind rather than prajna. Doesn't prajna understand the sense?

TRUNGPA RINPOCHE: Surprisingly not. That's the difference between prajna and *jnana*. Prajna understands the words completely, to the utmost extent that words can be understood. But to understand the sense, you have to develop jnana, wisdom. That's the whole point. That's why prajna corresponds to the sixth bhumi, or level, of the bodhisattva path, and you have to reach three levels beyond that before you develop jnana, wisdom. Prajna is not quite enough.

STUDENT: What happens to the aggression that characterizes or accompanies prajna when it reaches the level of shunyata?

TRUNGPA RINPOCHE: Aggression is still there in the form of intelligent energy. That still goes on: throughout the journey there will be a sense of energy, the excitement of new discovery. I suppose we could say that aggression becomes energy.

S: Does it level out and become less unbearable?

TR: There's no aggression as such. There's no question of a threshold of pain there. Aggression continues to be present somehow or other in the form of energy. After all, you still have your head. Even when you reach the *ati* level, you still carry your head with you. You know, you feel you have this thing with you. That kind of awareness is still there. It's very hard to clean up completely.

STUDENT: Where does buddha nature come into this?

TRUNGPA RINPOCHE: That is the essence, the fundamental essence of the wakeful quality, the thing that makes you struggle and proceed along the path. That appears right at the beginning and goes on all the way through. The other day I was talking about tantra as continuity and about the understanding of pain being the starting point of that continuity. That's the expression of buddha nature, which goes on constantly. There's actually a sense of threat connected with it, because you constantly have the potential of sanity.

S: And when you get to shunyata, that energy that is the driving force for the whole thing becomes just as it is, clear of all the other stuff around it?

TR: You don't have to be concerned about clearing away the other things. They just evaporate, so to speak, because you have such conviction, such real experience.

STUDENT: You said that prajna without shunyata was like a man without arms trying to climb a rock. Is the experience of shunyata like acquiring a pair of arms?

TRUNGPA RINPOCHE: Definitely, yes, because shunyata redefines compassion. Often compassion is spoken of in terms of the hook of compassion, like the sucker at the end of the tentacles of an octopus. The more arms you develop, the more powerful is the suction you develop at the same time. Shunyata is very much connected with building up compassion, warmth. So not only do you develop arms, but your arms become very functional.

STUDENT: You said in your first talk that we can never be happy and pain never ends. Is it true that in the shunyata experience, there is still pain, but there is no one to experience it, so it doesn't hurt?

TRUNGPA RINPOCHE: I think we could say that, yes. There will be pain if you are intelligent, but the hurting part or the seeking-for-pleasure part is a neurotic thing. With intelligence comes pain, but without neurosis there is no sorrow.

STUDENT: If the pain is no longer painful, what is there to distinguish between pain and pleasure?

TRUNGPA RINPOCHE: Very simple logic. In ordinary experience you can distinguish between coffee and tea. It's like that.

STUDENT: Shunyata for me always seems to have a huge connotation of desolation, but when you talk about it, it also seems to have fullness to it. What is that, or why is that?

TRUNGPA RINPOCHE: I suppose when you feel completely desolate, you begin to help yourself, you make yourself at home. You begin to realize all kinds of beauties around you. It's a question of identifying with the shunyata principle. That's why I said "make yourself at home."

STUDENT: Is it possible to confuse the shunyata experience with other levels of experience?

TRUNGPA RINPOCHE: I don't think so. Unless you are completely faking the shunyata experience to yourself, convincing yourself, hypnotizing yourself shunyata-style. Then obviously the whole thing becomes superficial. But at the level of the shunyata experience, you need your teacher much more, so that has a very grounding effect.

STUDENT: Is there a danger in pursuing the shunyata experience?

TRUNGPA RINPOCHE: Yes, very much so. The shunyata experience with ego is Rudrahood.

STUDENT: Is there an equivalent of the shunyata experience on the hinayana level?

TRUNGPA RINPOCHE: The only thing I can think of is the experience of impermanence, which is a glimpse of shunyata in a very literal sense—the all-pervasive feeling of nonexistence and impermanence—and of egolessness, for that matter, as well.

STUDENT: When you talked about expanding "this," it raised the question of Rudrahood for me. Then you said you could have a shunyata experience with ego. This makes me think I don't understand what "this" is.

TRUNGPA RINPOCHE: "This" is this [puts his hand on his chest], unmistakably. And "that" is ego, Rudra. "That" has a name, but "this" doesn't have a name.

STUDENT: Does the arhat experience shunyata?

TRUNGPA RINPOCHE: The experience of the arhat is not exactly shunyata as it is described in connection with the bodhisattva path. The arhat experiences a sense of egolessness, transitoriness within oneself. It doesn't even extend to objects like tables and chairs. It's just connected with the body and bodily sensations and the breath and emotions and thought patterns. It stops there and it doesn't expand, because there is very little warmth toward oneself at that point. There is very little emphasis on compassion. Since there is very little warmth, the arhat dwells only on his own problem and trying to solve that problem.

STUDENT: Rinpoche, what is the relationship of formal sitting practice to the shunyata experience? Is there any particular technique that would produce that experience?

TRUNGPA RINPOCHE: *Vipashyana* meditation automatically leads to shunyata. Also, sitting without any technique—just sitting—is shunyata practice. At that level, sitting practice becomes very ordinary and workable. There is quite possibly less struggle involved. Maybe there is just a hint of familiarity that makes it comfortable and easy to sit or to prolong one's sitting practice. But really there is no technique for shunyata. Such a thing would be a contradiction. Shunyata is just a way of being.

S: But would you say that having that experience is dependent upon practicing sitting meditation?

TR: Yes, I think so. There's no way out.

4

Beyond Shunyata

WE ARE GOING to discuss the basic meaning of going beyond shunyata. The walls of confusion and chaos are eliminated by prajna, and the ground of confusion and chaos is eliminated by the shunyata experience. Now we are suspended in midair. We have to learn how to walk, how to breathe, how to behave. That seems to be the next problem in the situation.

In the case of Naropa, he had decided to leave the monastery and search for Tilopa, but he still didn't know how to behave. Should he still behave like a pandit, a monk, a scholar? Or should he behave like an ordinary person searching for the truth? The answer to these questions is uncertain. Basic confusion is still there, and once again, self-consciousness. He did get the message of the shunyata lady, so to speak, but he does not know how to handle that. She did give him some hint about what to do, but beyond that everything is uncertain. How to go about working with that message is completely and totally uncertain for him.

The reason for this is that shunyata alone does not provide any guidance, even with skillful means. You still need a certain trust toward and respect for magic, the magical aspect of the phenomenal world. Things are very tricky. They are very tricky, and they play tricks on you spontaneously. There's nobody who is the game maker, who conceives of the game. Nobody's playing the tricks on you. But things as they are are full of trickery.

I suppose in the theistic tradition this might be called something like the mischievousness of God. But in the non-theistic tradition, the whole thing is not based on there being a maker of these tricks. The tricks that happen are tricks in themselves. That magical or miraculous quality of phenomenal display is always there. Particularly, it is always there when we feel we don't want to get into it, when we feel we haven't got time for it. When we are in a hurry to do something, something else happens. A trick is played on us that slows us down. And equally, when we are moved to relax and take our time, a trick is played on us that speeds us up. Such tricks happen constantly in our lives.

This is not hypothetical. This is something very real, extremely real, very definite.

Naropa resigns as abbot of Nalanda and goes to look for Tilopa. The voice of a trick says: "Tilopa is in the east. Go east, toward where the sun rises." Naropa does that, and he finds a leper woman blocking his path. Before encountering the leper woman, he thought he was finally going to meet Tilopa properly, meet the great master, the great guru, the enlightened Tilopa who could tell him the sense beyond the words. And before the leper woman disappears, we have this verse:

> Listen, Abhayakirti
> The Ultimate in which all become the same
> Is free of habit-forming thought and limitations.
> How, if still fettered by them,
> Can you hope to find the Guru?
>
> [p. 30]

There is a pattern in this odyssey, in this journey, which I thought I might relate to you. The eleven experiences [that follow his meeting with the ugly woman] seem to be divided into three sections. The first includes the leper woman, the bitch, the man playing tricks on his parents, and the man opening the body of the corpse. Those four are related to aggression. The next group is opening the stomach of the live man and washing it with hot water, marrying the king's daughter, and the huntsman. Those are connected with passion. The last group is connected with ignorance, a different type of temptation, a different kind of attempt to relate with reality that failed.

So, since Naropa was a scholar and a prajna type of person, obviously the first method he would use is that of aggression. The first experience in this category is an interesting one, a real demonstration of aggression. Seeing through the eyes [of prajna], Naropa has had a real vision, a real look at the experience of shunyata. This has made his mind much more vulnerable, so his aggression is coming out fast. He sees the leper woman with the sense of speed with which he is looking for his teacher. This is quite interesting and noteworthy.

The next thing is that he sees a bitch whose body is infested with worms. He thought he was just about to discover his guru Tilopa. Instead he sees this further expression of aggression—a bitch with the inside of her body crawling with worms. As the bitch is about to disappear, we have the verse:

All living beings by nature are one's parents.
How will you find the Guru, if
Without developing compassion
On the Mahayana path
You seek in the wrong direction?
How will you find the Guru to accept you
When you look down on others?

[pp. 30–31]

As we go along, these verses become progressively more tantric. The first section is very ordinary, very basic Buddhism. As we go on, things become deeper in many ways.

The next thing is the man playing tricks on his parents. Again Naropa fails to relate with himself. He still has the notion of being an articulate scholar from Nalanda, an accomplished leader, which makes him approach his search with a very genteel way of doing things. He has not yet gotten into the basic level of life. He hasn't actually related with father, mother, lover, enemy at all. A father and mother are related with the lover and enemy. The mother is the lover and the father is the enemy, the object of aggression. Since Naropa fails to relate with that, he has to journey further. As this particular vision is about to disappear, Tilopa says:

> How will you find the Guru, if
> In this doctrine of Great Compassion
> You do not crack the skull of egotism
> With the mallet of non-Pure-Egoness and
> nothingness?
>
> [p. 31]

The next one is the man opening the stomach of a corpse. This is a very powerful image, which has the sense that one should abandon the corpse that one is hanging on to. Nalanda University is a corpse for Naropa. He is trying to open that stomach again—trying to reevaluate himself by going through the library, so to speak, again and again. He still carries Nalanda with him as a tortoise carries his shell. He has to reeducate himself to the path of the yogi. As he is seeing this vision, Tilopa says:

> How will you find the Guru, if
> You cut not Samsara's ties
> With the unoriginatedness of the Ultimate
> In its realm of non-reference?
>
> [p. 32]

So that is the first section in which we have a glimpse of the fact that aggression comes from memory of the past. A person might be very proud of his past: "I was brought up in Brooklyn, so nobody can cheat me." Or in this case: "Nalanda is a very powerful place, the center of intelligence of the Indian empire, so no one can touch me." This same applies to the shunyata experience. You have been woken up by the ugly woman, and you still have that memory going on all the time in your state of being.

The next section, the section of passion, begins with the live man, who is a passionate live man who clings to life, which is a symbol of passion. Moreover, his stomach has been opened, which is more of a symbol of passion; there is a sense of the hot-blooded, the fleshy, live, warm. And his stomach is being washed in hot water, a further statement of passion, real passion. The basic message at this point is that Naropa is lacking enormously in compassion. He is treating the world like a shopping center rather than relating with himself. That has been his problem. All this mockery of Naropa comes because he is still shopping. He should look *into* himself and things more rather than looking for Tilopa as an external person. The verse at this point goes:

How will you find the guru, if
With the water of profound instruction
You cleanse not Samsara, which by nature [is] free
Yet represents the dirt of habit-forming thoughts?

[p. 32]

The basic theme of passion here has to do with the fact that Naropa still has to communicate with the world outside himself. On the other hand, he has been relating too much to this outsidedness as a shopping center in which Tilopa is the most valuable thing you can buy. He hasn't actually related with *himself* in order to communicate with the world. He hasn't spent a penny at this point. He's just been gazing at the whole universe. He has been fascinated by the world, but nothing has happened with his relationship with it. He is still roaming in the vacuums of shunyata.

This is much more than what we talk about as being "completely spaced out." We feel spaced out because we are spaced out [absent-minded]. Naropa feels completely spaced out because he has no reference point. In that condition, he can't even talk to anyone. He has no one to tell stories. He has no reference point at all. The whole thing is desolate and deathly in many ways.

In the next vision he sees the king, who asks him to marry his daughter. That's a very powerful thing. Considering that he is a fully ordained monk, this means he would have to break his vow. Breaking his vow at this point just means relating with the phenomenal world. Up till this point, he has built up an artificial virginity. And now he is breaking that virginity. Before he meets Tilopa, he should become Tilopa properly. He should be reduced to a garbage pile full of worms and flies, then burnt and reduced to dust. Having been reduced to dust, then he might receive instruction. That seems to be the point here. Marrying the king's daughter has nothing to do at all with the tantric teachings concerning the *karmamudra* or anything like that. It simply has to do with the fact that he is too clean, too slick, and he has to collect more dirt in order to become a really good and seasoned and antique student. In order to antique something, you put wax and dirt on it to make it look antique. So marrying the king's daughter is a process of seasoning. And Tilopa's verse here is:

Are you not deceived by a magic show?
How then will you find the Guru

If through desire and dislike you fall
Into the three forms of evil life?

[p. 32]

The next one is that Naropa meets a dark-skinned huntsman. The point here is exaggerated passion. Passion is usually
interpreted in terms of pleasure. Fulfilling passion is usually
related with attaining pleasure. But in this case it is also
connected with love and hate happening at the same time.
His journey has to stop at some point. He has to think twice
about himself. The verse here is:

A hunter, I have drawn the arrow
Of the phantom body which from desires is free
In the bow, of radiant light the essence:
I shall kill the fleeing deer of this and that,
On the mountain of the body believing in an I.
Tomorrow I go fishing in the lake.

[p. 33]

The next one is the old people plowing the field and eating
worms. This is the beginning of the ignorance section. This
section is related with the earth quality, earthiness. So it
begins with plowing the ground and eating worms, which are
also the product of earth. These are very earthy activities, but
equally freaky ones as far as Naropa is concerned. He probably
regarded ignorance as completely stupid and thought that
such ignorant people couldn't even plow or eat worms. But in
the case of this kind of intelligent ignorance, people *can* do
such things. The woman also cooks fish and frogs alive for
Naropa to eat. It is a kind of horrific idea that ignorance is so
alive and has managed to improvise all kinds of fantastic
things. And discovering this different version of ignorance is
like rediscovering himself. The verse here is:

Fettered by habit-forming thought, 'tis hard to
    find the Guru.
How will you find the Guru if you eat not
This fish of habit-forming thoughts, but hanker
After pleasures (which enhance the sense of ego)?
Tomorrow I will kill my parents.

[pp. 33–34]

Killing parents is one of the images of tantra. Now we are
getting closer to tantric images. Father is aggression, and
mother is passion. In many tantric vows, there are verses that
say, "Kill your father; make love to your mother." That's one
of the verses defining *samaya* discipline. It means to relate
with your father, aggression, completely, and your mother,
passion, completely. Get into them and relate with them. The
father is impaled and the mother is put in the dungeon. These
are expressions of aggression and passion, but at this point,
they are activities of ignorance. You might think that ignorance is just purely lying in the dungeon and being part of the
worms and so forth, but you begin to realize that this is not
so. There are very powerful things happening, *live* situations.
Ignorance has a living quality that is very prominent. Getting
into this is part of searching for the guru, actually being like
Tilopa. The verse here goes:

You will find it hard to find the Guru
If you kill not the three poisons that derive
From your parents, the dichotomy of this and that.
Tomorrow I will go and beg.

[p. 34]

These hints that begin with the huntsman saying, "Tomorrow I will do this or that," are interesting. Up to the point
where those begin, there is no need to sow a further seed of

confusion. Naropa is already confused. But after that point, it is necessary to sow a seed of confusion. You don't want to quite leave Naropa to himself so he can work things out completely. So the message about tomorrow sows a seed of expectation, and further confusion comes out of that. The method of teaching at this point is not designed to free Naropa or instruct him at all, but rather to confuse him more and more. That is the essence of the teaching style at this level, which is mahamudra.

The next one on the ignorance level is the beggar frying live fish and bringing dead fish back to life. He also asks Naropa to eat some live lice, which he hands him. Again, this conveys a sense of uncertainty. We could say that eating food is predominantly a mark of uncertainty. It's trying to make sure that we do have our body. We have food and drink when we are uncertain, when the boundaries become fuzzy. When that happens as we drive along on a highway, we decide to pull into a restaurant and eat. It's a way of reassuring ourselves. But eating live food is much more powerful than just stopping at a restaurant. You have to struggle to eat, because your food is struggling to get away from you. It is a very direct message, and at the same time quite horrific. The verses here are:

> If you would kill the misery of habit-forming
>   thoughts
> And ingrained tendencies on the endless path
> To the ultimate nature of all beings,
> First you must kill (these lice).
>
> [p. 35]

But when Naropa was unable to do so, the man disappeared with the words:

You will find it hard to find the Guru
If you kill not the louse of habit-forming
    thoughts,
Self-originated and self-destructive.
Tomorrow I will visit a freak show.

We shall do that tomorrow.

STUDENT: Did you say the "tomorrow" messages were designed to confuse Naropa?

TRUNGPA RINPOCHE: Yes.

S: I don't understand.

TR: They don't give any hint. At the beginning he was still carrying Nalanda University with him and was pretty much together. At that point, he had to be given some means for forgetting that memory. He had to be confused, given another kind of promise about his search for his Guru. He had to be lured into it more and at the same time made to forget his past hang-ups about Nalanda. So the way to confuse him was to lure him further in, as with the carrot and the donkey.

STUDENT: It seems that Naropa still has a big ego problem, even after the shunyata experience. You can still have ego, or these "habit-forming thoughts," even while you are experiencing shunyata?

TRUNGPA RINPOCHE: I think so. Much more so, in many ways. They become much more highlighted, I'm afraid. Or rather, I'm pleased to announce.

STUDENT: The effect of Naropa's marrying the king's daughter is to bring out more of his shit. Why doesn't the text say something to the effect: "You've got to relate more to your shit," rather than warning him about falling into the traps of samsara?

TRUNGPA RINPOCHE: That's the very clever thing about the whole business.

S: Is it sucking him further in that way?

TR: Of course. It's fantastic that way. The subject matter of all the songs, all the messages, is designed to confuse him. The messages are presented in accordance with certain moral patterns all the way. Even up to the highest mystical level, the messages still have a connection with that moral pattern. That's part of the masterpiece quality of this whole story.

STUDENT: When you say that the whole idea is to confuse him more, do you mean that strictly from ego's point of view? It's confusing ego?

TRUNGPA RINPOCHE: At this point it's all one. We can't really distinguish points of view. It's the point of view of the thing, the thingness.

S: It's not one person confusing another person?

TR: No, it's just the thing.

S: You mean like the tricks you were talking about?

TR: Yes. It's very tricky.

STUDENT: So the whole thing is just sucking him in all the way down the line. In that case, where does intelligence come in?

TRUNGPA RINPOCHE: At this point, his intelligence is being insulted rather than acknowledged in any way. Naropa had all kinds of intelligence, you know, and has been through all kinds of disciplines, but each time when he tries to pull any one of them out and use it, it is insulted.

STUDENT: By intelligence there, do you mean the—

TRUNGPA RINPOCHE: The prajna type.

STUDENT: No matter what Naropa did, would he be wrong? For example if the king offered him his daughter and he said, "No, I'm a monk, I can't take her," would the daughter disappear and say, "How can you find Tilopa if you don't accept the king's daughter?"

TRUNGPA RINPOCHE: No. It would be much longer than that. She would probably come out and seduce him. Then at the end she would say the same thing as the present verse does. The whole thing is a fantastic display of the greatest genius that one could ever think of. It's so apt.

STUDENT: It seems Naropa disarms himself with his motivation. He doesn't have any rebuttal for the insults to his intelligence because he's committed to pursuing Tilopa.

TRUNGPA RINPOCHE: He doesn't even think in terms of insults. He doesn't particularly think of discovery either at a certain point. Halfway through the search, before the "tomorrow" messages start coming, he has become dull and dumb and numb. That's the reason for the lines about "Tomorrow you'll see thus-and-such." They're to wake him up more. You don't want just to reduce him into a piece of lead. So the intention that runs through the messages is to keep him up, make him work harder.

STUDENT: Do those messages also tell him that although he's more confused than he was yesterday, he's making progress?

TRUNGPA RINPOCHE: Progress in terms of time and space but not in the amount of his understanding particularly.

S: At least he's getting another message.

TR: Yes, yes.

STUDENT: Is this by way of preparing a kind of a new ground for the meeting of Tilopa? Are all these temptations or confusions setting up a new ground to work with?

TRUNGPA RINPOCHE: Absolutely. Otherwise there's no point. You know, every one of these experiences provides fantastic ground to reflect back on and work on. It's a very ingenious strategy. And it doesn't particularly seem to be Tilopa personally who's doing it. Nobody knows who's doing it. If it had to be done in the ordinary way, the planning of how to handle Naropa would have taken ten years. It would be a million-dollar project in a university laboratory. And all the psychologists in the world would have to get together.

STUDENT: Is shunyata related to form being emptiness, and then is what's happening to Naropa in this later stage going back to the other side of emptiness being form?[1]

TRUNGPA RINPOCHE: I think so, yes.

STUDENT: Does this mean experiencing pain again in relationship with reality?

TRUNGPA RINPOCHE: Very much so. You get blissed out, so to speak, when you first discover shunyata. At that point Naropa got a message that he had a teacher, he had a guru. Now he's promised to seek his guru, and in that way he loses his ground. He's no longer walking on earth, he's walking on clouds. And those eleven experiences after the ugly woman bring him down and bring more pain, definitely. That's a kind of vajrayana type of pain that we've just barely discussed. And I think there's further pain just about to come.

STUDENT: You made the point several times that the sequence of situations is extremely apt and has been created by just the situations themselves. In terms of the personal application of this for any individual, is this a certain course that everyone on the path goes through? Is it that at a certain point in your development—after going through prajna and maybe having some first intuition of shunyata—situations will start having this confusing effect on people? Just from the situation, in a way that can't be duplicated, can't be made up? The effect does happen?

TRUNGPA RINPOCHE: I think so, yes. You seem to have got the feeling of the whole thing we have been discussing tonight. Sure.

STUDENT: In that sense is Naropa sort of like an everyman?

TRUNGPA RINPOCHE: By all means. If there weren't a sense of general application, we might be discussing this in some department of ethnic culture or some place like that. But we have decided to make it part of our study of American karma, which means that it does have some bearing on us, naturally. In fact, since you people decided to take part in this seminar, you have already inherited Naropa's sanity as well as his insanity, without any further choices. Welcome.

STUDENT: Is that a kind of confirmation?

TRUNGPA RINPOCHE: Well, what we're doing is a very minor confirmation.

S: No, I mean isn't the fact that the aptness of the message comes out of the situation itself a confirmation of some kind?

TR: I think so, yes.

STUDENT: Is the meeting with Vajrayogini a kind of archetypal meeting that's universal, that happens to all human beings at the first moment of giving up and letting go? Does that vision happen to most human beings at such a moment?

TRUNGPA RINPOCHE: I think so. It could happen in all kinds of ways. You might have an argument with your landlady or your mother-in-law. Every event like that is meeting the ugly woman. In this case, the ugly woman has nothing to do with male chauvinism. It's a cosmic thing. It's the cosmic principle of womanness. It would have to be a mother who cooks you food, or a girlfriend who bosses you around, or a secretary who minds your business. And every one of them is a cosmic principle and has nothing to do with male chauvinism at all. It's basic womanness in the highest sense.

STUDENT: Could you say something about Naropa noticing all the woman's marks of ugliness? Is it sort of another mockery of Naropa that he would catalogue all that?

TRUNGPA RINPOCHE: I think so, yes. Naropa hasn't reached the tenth bhumi. He's on the level of the sixth bhumi—prajna—and because his vision is not very clear, the woman is ugly. The less clear his vision, the more ugly the woman. Further on his vision becomes more refined. He has potential when he decides to seek Tilopa, but still his vision is very dull, so the ugly woman sharpens herself into further grotesque images like that of the leper woman and so forth.

S: What's the significance of her having all the ugly characteristics at that point?

TR: Those are the characteristics of samsara. Complete confusion, being trapped, being exploited, having your body torn apart, having parts of yourself eaten up, being stabbed, being dumped in shit, run over by a railroad train, being poisoned to death, stamped on, and all kinds of images. Those are the images of samsara. They say that the worst thing that could happen to you is being in samsara, that you will be completely annihilated in all kinds of ways—intellectually, spiritually, and socially; that you are the lowest of the lowest of the low. That's samsara. There's no fun in it.

STUDENT: Is Vajrayogini an aspect of Tilopa and vice versa?

TRUNGPA RINPOCHE: Vajrayogini is Tilopa's sister. She's a saleswoman, who awakens Naropa. It's like in Mexico you might find a boy that shines your shoes, and as he does it, he says, "Would you like to come and visit my sister's shop?"

5

Mahamudra

BEFORE WE DISCUSS Naropa's experiences with Tilopa further, we have to understand the meaning of mahamudra properly. So far we have only a very rough sketch of that experience. In our earlier discussion of continuity, we discussed it as starting from the level of the hinayana realization of pain and then going on to the shunyata experience. Then from the shunyata experience of emptiness, we are led to mahamudra. The sense of continuity there is rediscovering one's basic ground; the mahamudra experience could be described that way. Having had all the illusions and hallucinations removed by the experience of shunyata, there is a sense of extraordinary clarity. That clarity is called mahamudra.

Mahamudra is a Sanskrit word. *Maha* means "big, great," and *mudra* means "symbol." But *maha* doesn't mean "big" in a comparative sense: something bigger compared to something smaller. It is not based on a dichotomy. It is simply that such clarity as this is beyond measure. There is no other clarity like this. It is fullness; it is without association in the sense that this experience is full in itself. And the sense in which *mudra* means symbol again has nothing to do with analysis or examples; rather the thing itself is its own symbol. Everybody represents themselves and everybody is a caricature of themselves. There is that sense of a humorous aspect, a caricature aspect, as well as everything having its own basic fullness. You represent yourself not by name but by being. So there is a sense of completion.

The mahamudra experience has been compared to the experience of a young child visiting a colorful temple. He sees all kinds of magnificent decorations, displays, rich colors, vividness of all kinds. But this child has no preconception or any concept whatsoever about where to begin to analyze. Everything is overwhelming, quite in its own right. So the child does not become frightened by this vivid scenery and at the same time does not know how to appreciate it. It is quite different from a child walking into a playroom full of toys, where his attention is caught by a particular toy and he runs right over and starts playing with it. A temple, a highly decorated, colorful temple, is so harmonious in its own right that the child has no way of introducing his fascination from one particular standpoint. The experience is all-pervasive. At the same time it is perhaps somewhat overwhelmingly pleasurable.

So the mahamudra experience is vividness, vividness to such an extent that it does not require a watcher or commentator; or for that matter it does not require meditative absorption. In the case of shunyata, there is still a sense of needing a nursing process for that experience; it is not only that the sitting practice of meditation is required, but there is a sense of needing a registrar to record your experience in a memory bank. The very idea of emptiness is an experience, even though you may not have an experienc*er* as such, since the whole thing is totally open and nondualistic. But even the very sense of nonduality is a faint stain, a very subtle, transparent stain. On the shunyata level, that stain is regarded as an adornment, like putting a varnish over well-finished wood. It is supposed to protect the wood from further stains of dirt or grease, to keep it looking fresh and new, to preserve the newness of this well-finished wood. But in the long run, that clear varnish becomes a factor that ages the new look of this fresh wood. It turns yellow and begins slowly to crumble, and scratches begin to show much more in it than they would in the original wood. So the nonduality becomes a problem in the shunyata experience.

In the experience of mahamudra, even the notion of non-duality is not applied, or is not necessary. Therefore, it has been said in the scriptures that the only definition of maha-mudra you can use is "unborn" or "unoriginated." Or again, often the mahamudra experience is described in terms of coemergent wisdom—that is, born simultaneously rather than born with the delays of process. This refers to confusion and realization existing simultaneously, as opposed to confusion coming first and then realization taking over and cleaning out the confusion. In the mahamudra, confusion and realization are simultaneous, coemergent.

The eternally youthful quality of the mahamudra experience is one of its outstanding qualities. It is eternally youthful because there is no sense of repetition, no sense of wearing out of interest because of familiarity. Every experience is a new, fresh experience. So it is childlike, innocent and childlike. The child has never even seen its body—such a brand-new world.

Another term for mahamudra, used by Rangjung Dorje and other great teachers, is "ordinary consciousness." Experience ceases to be extraordinary. It is so ordinary—so clear and precise and obvious. The only thing that confuses us and prevents us from realizing this experience is its ordinariness. The ordinary quality becomes a kind of barrier, because when you look for something, you don't look for the ordinary. Even in the case of losing a pair of glasses that you are completely used to. When you lose them, the glasses become a very interesting object. They immediately become an extraordinary thing, because you lost them. You begin to imagine: "Could they be here? Could they be there?" You shake all the cushions, you move all the chairs and tables, and look underneath the rugs. It becomes an extraordinary case. But the glasses are an ordinary thing.

In that way, mahamudra is self-secret because of its ordinariness. Ordinariness becomes its own camouflage, so to speak. It has also been said that mahamudra cannot be expressed, that even the Buddha's tongue is numb when it comes to describing mahamudra. And it's true. How much can you say about ordinary things? And the more you see that it is very ordinary, the more that becomes an extraordinary case, which creates a further veil.

The experience of mahamudra is also somewhat irritating, or even highly irritating, because of its sharpness and precision. The energies around you—textures, colors, different states of mind, relationships—are very vivid and precise. They are all so naked and so much right in front of you, without any padding, without any walls between you and that. That nakedness is overwhelming. Although it is your own experience, we often find that even when you have only a small glimpse of mahamudra experience, you want to run away from yourself. You look for privacy of some kind—privacy from yourself. The world is so true and naked and sharp and precise and colorful that it's extraordinarily irritating—let alone when other *people* approach you. You think you can avoid them, run away from them physically, put a notice on your door, or take a trip to an unknown corner of the world. You might try to dissociate yourself from the familiar world, run away from your home ground, disconnect your telephone. You can do all kinds of things of that nature, but when the world begins to become *you* and all these preceptions are *yours* and are very precise and very obviously right in front of you, you can't run away from it. The process of running away creates further sharpness, and if you really try to run away from these phenomena, they begin to mock you, laugh at you. The chairs and tables and rugs and paintings on the wall and your books, the sounds you hear in your head, begin to mock you. Even if you try to tear your body apart, still something follows you. You can't get away from it. That is why it is called the ultimate nakedness. You begin to feel you are just a live brain with no tissue around it, exposed on a winter morning to the cold air. It's *so* penetrating, irritating, and so sharp.

It is a fundamental and very profound irritation. The irritations we discussed before are relatively simple and seem to be ordinary ones. The irritation of the mahamudra experience is very insulting in many ways, disconcerting. That is why the experience of mahamudra is also referred to as "crazy wisdom." It is a crazy experience, but not exactly ego madness. It's wisdom that has gone crazy. The element of wisdom here is its playfulness, humorousness, and its sybaritic quality. Even though you are irritated and naked and completely exposed without your skin, there is a sense of joy, or more likely, bliss.

One of the definite characteristics of the Buddhist tantra, on the mahamudra level at least, is not running away from sense pleasures, but rather identifying with them, working with them as part of the working basis. That is an outstanding part of the tantric message. Pleasure in this case includes every kind of pleasure: psychosomatic, physical, psychological, and spiritual. Here it is quite different from the way in which spiritual materialists might seek pleasure—by getting into the other. In this case, it is getting into "this." There is a self-existing pleasurableness that is completely hollow if you look at it from the ordinary point of view of ego's pleasure orientation. Within that, you don't actually experience pleasure at all. All pleasure experiences are hollow. But if you look at it from the point of view of this nakedness, this situation of being completely exposed, any pleasure you experience is full because of its hollowness. On the mahamudra level, pleasure does not take place through the pores of your skin, but pleasure takes place on your very *flesh* without skin. You become the bliss rather than enjoying the bliss. You are the embodiment of bliss, and this contains a quality of your being very powerful. You have conquered pleasure, and pleasure is yours. One doesn't even have to go so far as to try to enjoy pleasure, but pleasure becomes self-existing bliss.

In this way every experience that might occur in our life— communication, visual experience, auditory experience, consciousness: anything that we relate to—becomes completely workable, highly workable. In fact, even the notion of workability does not apply. It's yours. It is *you,* in fact. So things become very immediate.

This is what is often called vajra pride. Pride in this case is not arrogance, but is nondualistically self-contained. You are not threatened by your projections or projectors, but you are there, and at the same time everything around you is you and yours.

It took a long time for Naropa to realize that. Having visited the freak show, he failed again. Finally, at the last moment, when he thought of killing himself and was just about to relate with the totality of himself, *finally* then he experienced that penetrating pain in himself. He thought that maybe if he eliminated his body, he might be able to relieve that pain. At that point, Tilopa finally appeared. Through the twelve tortures that Naropa went through (with the help of Tilopa), sometimes he understood this nakedness, experiencing it fully, totally, completely, and sometimes he didn't understand it and instead tripped out into the highest spiritual mishmash. The perfect example is when Tilopa put sharpened pieces of bamboo between his nails and his fingers, and put little flags on the ends of the pieces of bamboo, and asked Naropa to hold them up into the wind. That exemplifies

(through the medium of pain, of course) how real the nakedness could be if it were blissful.

That seems to be a very powerful message for us. Mind you,
we are not going to practice that very exercise with every
student, but that is an example of what the process is like.
How many times can the guru tell a person, "Come out! I
know you're there! Be naked!" A student might decide to take
off his clothes and say, "Okay, I'm naked," but that's not
quite it. We have to say: "There's more nakedness. Come on,
do more than that. What else can you do?"

Particularly a scholar like Naropa had enormous hang-ups.
Receiving instructions from a mahayana teacher requires only
simple devotion, reducing oneself to an infant and asking the
guru to act as the babysitter. But on the vajrayana level, the
student-teacher relationship demands more than that. It is a
process of training the student as a warrior. At first, a warrior
teacher does not use a sword on you. He uses a stick and
makes you fight with him. Since the student's swordsmanship
is not so good, he gets hurt more than he is able to hurt the
master. But when the student gains confidence and begins to
learn good swordsmanship, he is almost able to defeat his own
teacher. Then instead of a stick it becomes a sword. Nobody
really gets killed or hurt, because all the levels of communication take place within the realm of the rainbow or mirage
anyway. But there is a training period. A learning process
takes place, which is very immediate and very powerful and
very necessary.

On the hinayana level, the teacher is a wise man. On the
mahayana level, he is a physician/friend, a spiritual friend. On
the vajrayana level, the student-teacher relationship is similar
to that in the martial arts. You could get hurt severely if you
are too tense. But you could also receive a tremendous—
almost physical—message. The message is not verbal or intellectual. It is like a demonstration of putting tables and chairs

together. The teachings come out of the world of form, the real world of form. The teachings consist of colors and forms and sounds rather than words or ideas.

This is what Naropa was going through—the physical teachings, which are real and direct and obvious. And they are personal, highly personal. Each time we come closer to tantra in the journey through the *yanas,* the relationship to the teacher changes and becomes more and more personal. The teacher acts as his own spokesman but also as the spokesman of the vivid and colorful world that you are part of. If you don't have the experience of winter, you have to take off your clothes and lie in the snow at night. That way you will learn a very good lesson on what winter is all about that doesn't need words. You could read a book about it, but it doesn't mean very much unless you have that very immediate and direct experience—which is frightening, very powerful.

Somehow we are unable to have an experience of this nature without going through the basic learning process that enables you to handle that kind of experience. Therefore the three-yana principle is very important—the gradual process from hinayana to mahayana to vajrayana. This process makes it all make sense. Without it, it does not make any sense; it is just training in masochism.

There's a story about a certain workshop that took place in this country, I don't remember exactly where. It was supposed to be a workshop in self-exposure, and anybody interested in that workshop could just pay their money and come in, without having the faintest idea what it was all about. They were invited to eat dinner together. There was beautifully prepared food and nice china and a nice tablecloth and candlelight and everything. They ate their food and they drank their wine. Then at the end of the meal, everybody was supposed to break their plates and glasses and chop up their tables and chairs. That was the workshop. What does it mean?

Of course it might mean a lot if you really know what it is all about. But on the other hand, if you just saw that advertised in the newspaper and decided to go to it because you thought it was a groovy thing to do—you'd never done *that* before—it wouldn't mean very much. You might feel uncertain how much you should talk to the others about the experience. You might feel slightly awkward and at the same time released or something or other. But on the whole it would make no sense if there were no training process behind it.

Vajrayana is also very powerful, but you can't just come in and do the workshop of the twelve trials of Naropa. It doesn't mean anything without basic training in mindfulness, awareness, groundlessness, and fearlessness. In that sense tantra is a very dangerous thing. At the same time, it is very powerful, and every one of us can do it. Other people have done so. Actually, we don't have to be such great scholars as Naropa was. As long as we are interested in using our intellect and our intuition, we can do it. Mahamudra is possible as long as we have some basic training in relating with ourselves. We have to learn fearlessness that is without hesitation but is not based on blind faith. If we have a logical mind, a scientific mind full of suspicion, that is good.

STUDENT: Why do you tell us all this? I find this kind of explosion quite frightening.

TRUNGPA RINPOCHE: That's good. It means you're beginning to feel it.

S: Yes, I am.

TR: That's good. It's not up to me to keep this a secret. You might develop your own self-secretness your own way of keeping it a secret from yourself. But if you're afraid, that means something is cooking. That's good to hear.

STUDENT: Is mahamudra the first point at which the idea of

samsara and nirvana ceases to apply? Or does that happen back with shunyata?

TRUNGPA RINPOCHE: In shunyata, there is the idea of the nonduality of samsara and nirvana, but there is still a sense of this being sacred. In mahamudra, there is definitely nonexistence of samsara and nirvana.

STUDENT: You said that at the point in the student-teacher relationship where sticks are exchanged for swords, that all communication takes place in a rainbow realm. I was wondering if you could explain that a little more.

TRUNGPA RINPOCHE: At the point where you pick up swords, there is no gain and no loss. At the level of using sticks, there may be still gain and loss, but when you pick up the swords, there's no gain and no loss.

S: Couldn't it be a very great loss if you got your head cut off?

TR: Well, your head is not particularly a concern here. The point is that you become a highly skilled dancer. You and the teacher can still play together even if you have no head. That's what I mean by rainbow.

S: How is that a rainbow?

TR: That's the rainbow. The teacher can still train a student without a head, or a student can learn without the head that's been chopped off. The physical, literal situation does not apply there anymore. It's as transparent as the rainbow, yet it is still colorful and vivid.

STUDENT: You said that in the shunyata experience, ego is still a problem. Is the ego still a problem in mahamudra?

TRUNGPA RINPOCHE: In the mahamudra experience, ego is not a problem, but the memory of the previous yana is a problem. You have to recover from the hangover of the previous medicine you were taking.

S: The previous medicine was shunyata?

TR: Yes. It works that way throughout the rest of the yanas. Throughout the tantric yanas, it works that way.

S: So in the shunyata experience there is still an element of duality between ego and—

TR: An element of nonduality. That's the problem.

S: Oh, yes. I see.

STUDENT: What's the difference between the pain we experience at first and the pain we experience in mahamudra?

TRUNGPA RINPOCHE: The difference is that this pain is much, much more real. It is direct pain that is beyond any neurosis. The other one is seeming pain, psychosomatic pain.

S: You mean earlier on you don't get into the pain?

TR: That's right.

STUDENT: You said at one point that ego is pain and pain is ego. If you lose your ego, how can you experience pain?

TRUNGPA RINPOCHE: The absence of ego is pain still. You still feel the absence of ego, nonduality.

S: So that's still an experience.

TR: That has been compared to an empty perfume bottle. You can still smell the perfume.

STUDENT: You said that mahamudra was unoriginated, but then you said that confusion and realization come about at the same time. It sounds like something is originating.

TRUNGPA RINPOCHE: Well, they don't help each other;

they don't ferment each other. They are just unoriginated; they come out of nowhere.

STUDENT: Does the bodhisattva ideal of service to other sentient beings extend over into vajrayana?

TRUNGPA RINPOCHE: Basically, yes; but on the vajrayana level, it is less pious and more immediate. On the mahayana level, there is still a notion of doing good.

STUDENT: Could people experience mahamudra through taking acid? It seems to me that that is possible, but, as you said before, without the proper preparation it wouldn't make any sense.

TRUNGPA RINPOCHE: You said it. You see, the mahamudra experience has nothing to do with being high. It's very real and direct. You are no longer under the control of the other. You are just yourself, very simply. But any kind of hallucinogenic experience has a sense of the other.

S: You mean memory, comparison to other experience?

TR: Yes.

STUDENT: You said that mahamudra pain was without neurosis, and you also said that in the rainbow realm you could cut your head off and still learn. I am a little confused about what is going on here. What is direct pain at that level? Can it be talked about?

TRUNGPA RINPOCHE: Pain from having your head chopped off. You have no head, right? But you still have a headache. That kind of pain.

S: Is that physiological or psychosomatic?

TR: Well, obviously psychosomatic. When I talk about your head being chopped off, I do not mean that the vajrayana master and his student would literally have swordplay. That's a figurative thing. That pain is very immediate pain. When you have no head, you still get a very painful headache. It becomes very penetrating.

STUDENT: You were talking about the relationship between master and student in the vajrayana being personal. I was wondering how one makes it get personal.

TRUNGPA RINPOCHE: The whole style of teaching is personal. The teacher minds your business forever. It's not necessarily a matter of the teacher's physical presence, having a constant relationship with your teacher physically present. But whenever the teaching is given to you, the means, methods, and techniques of conveying the teaching are very personal.

STUDENT: Is it that on the vajrayana level, you yourself become an embodiment of your spiritual friend?

TRUNGPA RINPOCHE: It's more that the guru is like a pill that you swallow that always remains in your stomach. Either it could poison and kill you on the spot or it could grant you everlasting life. It's very personal. One of the basic principles of the vajrayana is what is called the *samaya* vow. The guru sows a seed in you which is part of himself, and you have that seed in you, and the guru has remote control of that seed.

STUDENT: In Naropa's acts of self-denial, there is that repeated formula in which Tilopa says something like, "If I had a disciple wanting instruction, he would (for example) jump into the fire." Then Naropa does it and almost gets killed every time. I don't understand why he does that. Is it that he is still clinging to his ego?

TRUNGPA RINPOCHE: It's something more than ego. It's

that he has to become more naked. He is still not unmasking enough. It's more a process of stripping than of giving up ego—which he has already done anyway. Each one of his acts seems to be an enormous example of surrendering ego. But after surrendering his ego, he also has to unmask properly.

STUDENT: You said that the mahamudra experience is irritating because of its nakedness, very irritating. Then later you said that in the mahamudra realm, you are bliss. My approach may be very dualistic, but for me irritation and bliss don't go together.

TRUNGPA RINPOCHE: Irritation happens at the level when you are still ambitious, when you are first committing yourself to the mahamudra path and you are beginning to see new views of the world. Seeing new views is very irritating. It's like, in the middle of a sunny day in Greece, taking off your dark glasses. The glare is so irritating to your eyes. And that's the first experience. But then you get used to it, and you learn to perceive things without distortion. And that becomes bliss. So it's a gradual process. Irritation comes first. Things are so close to heart, so immediate. Then you become used to it and develop confidence. Then the whole thing becomes bliss.

STUDENT: How is assimilating the teacher as a pill or a seed different from taking a drug? How do you get rid of the sense of the teacher as the other?

TRUNGPA RINPOCHE: Well, drugs don't last very long, and the teacher lasts your whole life.

S: But is the sense of the teacher always there?

TR: Until you become a teacher yourself.

STUDENT: Are the other visions that Naropa had after the

old lady's shadow fell on his book and before he met Tilopa also manifestations of shunyata?

TRUNGPA RINPOCHE: Yes. Very much so.

S: But it seems that they're so concrete, that their whole point is somehow this concreteness. How is that connected with shunyata as emptiness?

TR: It's because of its fullness. The fullness does not allow any room; therefore that frozen space could be called empty space.

S: Then how does that fullness lead into the fullness of mahamudra?

TR: Mahamudra is very sharp, not just full alone. It's colorful. Shunyata fullness is rather gray and transparent and dull, like London fog. But the mahamudra experience of fullness is humorous; it is also the fullness of little particles dancing with each other within the fullness. It's like a sky full of stars and shooting stars and all the rest—so many activities are taking place.

6

The Levels of Mahamudra

THERE ARE DIFFERENT levels of mahamudra, which are related to different levels of clarity. Clarity here means confidence and fearlessness, rather than being a purely phenome-
nological quality.

According to the Buddhist approach, advancement toward
enlightenment does not come from insight alone but also from
skillful means. On the bodhisattva path, a powerful skillful
means is the practice of the six *paramitas*—working with other
sentient beings. In the vajrayana, exchange with the world is
also a means of development. That seems to be a general
pattern. In the vajrayana experience of mahamudra, first one
develops one's basic sanity, and having done that, the only
way to grow up and mature further is through further openness
to the world. That is one of the important elements.

In order to relate with the world, one has to develop
confidence. In order to develop confidence, one has to have
some level of identification with one's basic being. As a result,
at this stage the five buddha principles become very prominent. You begin to develop an affinity with a particular buddha
principle through receiving an *abhisheka,* or initiation, from a
vajra master, that is, a vajrayana teacher. That vajra master,
or teacher, teaches one how to conduct oneself as a real
practitioner of the vajrayana. He is also the example one can
follow. The key point is the meeting of his mind and your
mind, together with the mutual discovery of a particular

mandala. In this case the mandala is a host of deities, which are associated with one's basic being. That is to say, the deities represent your type of energy rather than being divine beings who are external separate entities or even internal separate entities. At the moment of the discovery of this mandala, your own basic beingness is discovered in an enlightened form— the Jack-ness or the John-ness of you. Your basic beingness is seen in an enlightened form, in a mahamudra form. You begin to see that. You develop, not fascination, but an identification with such principles, which have your own particular characteristics, which are those of a particular buddha family: *vajra, ratna, padma, karma, buddha.*

The point of this is realization of the sacredness of the universe and of yourself. There are different ways of viewing sacredness. One might think: The world is sacred because it was created by God, and the mysteriousness of God and His power and all-pervasiveness are beyond mind's measure. They boggle the mind, they're beyond our limited capacity. And because they are beyond the measure of our small mind, they should be regarded as divine principles. Since we don't have the power or the knowledge to make a rock, since we couldn't invent planets or create the four seasons, since that is beyond our control and reflects such power, it is unthinkable, and therefore sacred. No one could conquer this large Conductor of the universe. Only God is on that level. By associating with this great principle, you might be helped to become one with it, but that is questionable; it depends on how good you are.

Another approach to sacredness might also be connected with meditative absorption. If you succeed in developing meditative absorption, you tend to get an ineffable experience of something-or-other. You can't name it. It is associated with divine power. One connects it with how He created the universe. It's beyond words, beyond concept.

The approach of vajrayana Buddhism to sacredness has a

different quality. It is not so much a matter of things being big and enormous and beyond the measure of one's thought; rather it has to do with things being so true, so real, so direct. We know a fire burns. We know the earth carries us. We know that space accommodates us. All these are *real* facts, and so obvious. Obviousness becomes sacredness from the point of view of vajrayana. It is not that things are sacred because they are beyond our imagination, but because they are so obvious. The magic is simplicity. Winter gets cold, summer gets warm. Everything in every situation has a little magic. If we forget to eat, we get hungry. There is a causal aspect, which is the truth. So in this case, the sacredness is a matter of truth, of the obviousness of the whole thing.

This has nothing particular to do with how things happen to be *made,* but rather how they *are.* There's no reference to the past in vajrayana, no concern with the case history of things, or with chronology. The concern is with *what is.* When we look at things as they are on a very simple and ordinary level, we find that they are fantastically, obviously true, frighteningly true. Because of their quality of being true and obvious, things are sacred and worth respecting. This kind of truth reveals falsity automatically. If we are slightly off the point, we get hit or pushed or pulled. We get constant reminders, constant help. It's that kind of sacredness.

Another part of sacredness is a sense of well-being, which is a very interesting thing. It is a very typical characteristic of the vajrayana approach. This sense of well-being has to do with the fact that although you might be awe-struck by the penetrating truth and obviousness of things, at the same time, in spite of this awesome quality, there is no sense of threat. There is a sense of courtship, of a love affair between the obviousness and you perceiving it.

The obstacle to this well-being is naiveté or mindlessness. Things are taken for granted; things are never questioned, never looked at. The sense of well-being has a quality of appreciation. You appreciate that you possess, or are in, such a beautiful universe, that the universe is part of you and you are part of it.

The mahamudra experience of clarity and sharpness allows us to develop a new attitude in which things are never taken for granted, in which every moment is a new experience. With that sense of sacredness, of well-being, one begins to rediscover the universe. Since this is not a fantasy but a real experience, it cannot be destroyed. As much doubt as comes up, that is how much clarity shines through. Because of this, this experience is called vajra, a Sanskrit word which means "adamantine" or "indestructible." Even the threat of defeat of this vajra quality is used as fuel for it to maintain itself. Therefore, it is constantly indestructible, imperturbable.

In the vajrayana practice of performing the *sadhanas* of the particular *yidams* who are appropriate to you that were given to you by your teacher, you identify with the iconographical representation of a yidam. Identifying with the iconographical details is no longer a problem, because you know the basic characteristics of the deity, and you have a sense of that in your mind already. Probably we would have no problem at all visualizing Uncle Sam, because we know what Uncle Sam represents. The image is very vivid. It is a similar kind of thing when you are given the practice of a particular deity and mandala. If you have a complete and thorough understanding of it, then it is no longer foreign or alien but easy to recognize and identify with.

Still, visualization is very tricky. It is not just fingerpainting your imaginations in your mind. It's getting into the spirit of what you're visualizing. Take as an example visualizing Broadway in New York City in the early evening. You close your eyes and begin to see yellow cabs and other traffic and neon lights and buildings and people walking. You visualize it completely. You don't actually have to visualize it; you just switch your mind to it and automatically you are there. You feel as though you are in New York City already, so you don't have to pay too much attention to details. You don't have to think about how many lampposts there are on Broadway or what color the neon lights are, particularly. You just get a sense of the general proportions and the general climate.

So that's the approach to visualization, rather than imagining an alien-looking guy with three heads and twelve arms, who turns into something plastic rather than a deity. Because if you don't have a real sense of who the deities are and what they represent, then visualization becomes just a child's game.

In tantric practice, there is the notion that sights, sounds, and consciousness turn into the expressions of those deities. Sight, or visual objects, become part of the realm of the deity, and sounds become the deity's mantra, and the thought process, or consciousness, becomes the wisdom of the deity. This does not mean that everybody appears dressed up as a deity, and that everyone's conversations are in the form of mantra, and that everybody's mind is blissed out. Rather, what you see has the quality of a particular deity. The principle is all-pervasive because it is your principle. You can't see any other world than your world, and sight, sound, and thought process becomes a part of that style. Then it becomes very vivid. At a certain point, even if you would like to forget about this or it becomes too much for you, it still follows you. That awareness comes back to you by itself rather than your having to try to be aware of it. This kind of identification with your basic principle, the awakening of your basic principle, is the starting point for developing confidence at the beginning. This is very important, extraordinarily important.

When you have achieved this confidence and dignity, the awareness is not constant all the time, but hundreds of flashes of awareness happen to you instantaneously. At that point, probably it is time to extend your practice out into relating with your exterior, with your expressions. So far you have been working with your *im*pressions, with your interior. Now you are going to work outward into the exterior, which is composed of all kinds of states of being. The first thing is to arouse energy. At that point, you still have all kinds of neurotic leftovers remaining, so you have to have a way of utilizing those leftovers as part of the energy. You also have to destroy any sense of preserving your perceptions of sight and sound and so on. Destroying that sense of preservation is a giving-away process.

This is where the first dharma of Naropa, called tumo, comes in. You may have heard of this. It does not simply mean developing central heating within your body so that you don't have to depend on warm clothes. It's not quite as utilitarian as that—or as cheap as that. *Tumo* is a Tibetan word that means "wrathful one." *Tum* means "wrath" or "anger"; *mo* is a feminine ending, so it is "female wrathful one." This is related to what is called *chandali* in Sanskrit, which is "flame" or "energy." But one cannot develop the physical effects of this practice until one has conquered or destroyed the sense of preserving one's being. One is consumed by this flame of chandali, which has no compassion that goes in only one direction. Because it *is* compassion, it does not require any extra compassion. It is an all-consuming flame.

Then one does get the physical result of not being at the mercy of the elements. If you are in a hot country, you feel cool. If you are in a cool country, you feel warm. But that seems to be beside the point. The point here is dealing with the tension that one builds up within one's being, a psycho-somatic tension that creates a sense of weakness. The body becomes such a big deal that one does not want to endure even the smallest discomfort. There is tremendous fear involved. Even the littlest discomfort brings enormous panic, particularly when you begin to think that you can't renew the body, you can't get further supplies to keep yourself happy. So there's a sense of panic, which is the cause of tension. One becomes very tight; psychosomatically, one's whole body becomes one lump of muscle. This makes one very vulnerable to the elements—the psychosomatic or the physical elements. This sense of tension—or anger—creates enormous unnecessary suffering.

Then there is the next dharma of Naropa, realization of the illusory body. Having disowned one's body, having conquered one's sense of possessiveness toward one's body, one's being, one's ego, then one begins to mingle oneself with the rest of the mirage of sounds, colors, shapes, energies, emotions—everything. Mingling with that is the practice of illusory body. It's a kind of celebration. Constantly, there is joy, a dance taking place. It's not to maintain your thing, but to celebrate.

Then there is the next dharma, dream. This is not necessarily dream at the level of sleep. It is the dreams that we have all the time in our lives, the fantasies and real experiences of our life during the day, the fantasies and thought processes that make our life like it is happening in Disneyland. The search for entertainment is an important aspect of the dream activity. If you realize the dream as dream, then there is no entertainment. But that does not necessarily mean depression. Entertainment is the sense of getting your money's worth, so to speak, or your energy's worth. But if we realize dream as dream the whole approach to life becomes less businesslike, but at the same time very practical. Relating with friends, relatives, the business world, enemies—all these experiences become more real. Generally we think of dreams differently; we think of dreams as something unreal and of something that is not dreams as real. That seems to be a misunderstanding. The point of the dream yoga is to free oneself from the

Disneylandlike quality, which is our regular day life, and replace that with dream experience, which is real life. From that point of view, if one could live completely in the dream world, that would be much more real and pragmatic and efficient and complete than the so-called nondream world.

Luminosity is the next one, light. That is a further elaboration of the intelligence one should develop in the *real* dream state, in which you don't dream but you live properly. There is a sense of panoramic awareness. You are certain about how things function. There is the confidence that we have already developed: the sense of real, genuine understanding and awareness, which is the absence of threat. That is the experience of luminosity.

The next one is called *phowa* in Tibetan, which literally means "pass out" or "eject." In this case, it's more likely "eject." This means that you are capable of making your consciousness step outside of your body when the time comes. Or your consciousness can enter into another body when the time comes. This again means cutting through a lot of possessiveness toward one's body, particularly the desire for possessions and entertainment. One has to have the power to remove clingings. You can step out in the middle of your meal; before you finish your sentence, you can step out. You don't have a chance to finish your pun or to finish your dessert. You have to leave things behind, which can be very scary and very unsatisfying.

The last one has to do with sleep.[1] There was an Indian siddha called Lavapa who fell asleep for twelve years by the side of the main highway running through his city. At the end of twelve years, he had realized mahamudra completely. Sleep is both literal and symbolic here. Symbolically, there is the sense that the samsaric state is a state of deep sleep. Also, physical sleep is a state of complete unconsciousness before dreams arise. The idea is to develop complete awareness, or better in this context of mahamudra, a state of wakefulness. When you're awake, you don't have to make a point of being aware, because you are constantly awake in any case. You can do other things along with that. That is the real example of mahamudra; mahamudra is like being awake; you don't have to maintain your practice or state of wisdom. Everything functions simply and naturally within the process of being awake.

Traditionally, after completing the six dharmas of Naropa, a person begins to practice hatha yoga—*pranayama* and so forth. The final outcome of the yoga practices is that you learn to perform miracles. Relating with the body in a certain way is very magical. Thus it is regarded as very dangerous to introduce hatha yoga, or playing with your breath, or whatever, at too early a stage. You still don't have intelligence, awareness, and confidence functioning in a coordinated way. Everything is not synchronized properly. The danger and the strain come when this synchronization does not exist but you are still pushing to achieve.

The notion of miracle is very interesting. Here miracle is something very basic. It has to come about through the karmic situation, what is going on in your life and in the life of your country. Certain very powerful coincidences take place, and you might become the instigator of them. But if your action is not attuned to the karmic situation, things will go wrong. For instance, if you have the magical power to produce anything you want, the obvious first thing you might do is produce lots of bank notes. But that would create a strange fluctuation in the economic world. The bank notes you've produced won't have been registered properly; though they are seemingly real, they are actually fake. Your action becomes criminal. Somehow the whole thing has to work with the karmic situation that exists in your country. You can't over-saturate the market. So a miracle is not one-sided in character.

It is a mutual creation of you and the situation in the country. The country's energy and yours become the instigator.

The idea of hatha yoga practice is also to relate with the elements properly, make friends with them—the physical elements as well as the psychological elements. In other words, the vajrayana process is getting to know the world in the fullest possible way. By doing that, you will be able to work with other people and help them, because they are part of this universe, and they have their connections to the elements as well.

STUDENT: Can you say anything more about stepping out, which you spoke of in connection with phowa practice?

TRUNGPA RINPOCHE: It's being willing to leave. Things are half-finished, and there is a desire to finish them. You have a sense of openness that gives you the power to step out anytime you wish. That can also extend to being able to step out of your body, leave your body whenever you wish. But the situation has to be right. You can't practice phowa if you're freaking out and regarding it as a suicidal thing. In that case, you would still be kept in your body, because you would have a sense of imprisonment. The greater your sense of imprisonment, the more surely you will be kept in your body. So it would not work if you approached it suicidally. It's a sense of letting go.

S: Is it to be practiced at the time of death?

TR: Yes, but not only. It should have implications in all directions.

STUDENT: Rinpoche, you seem to be saying that visualization of buddhas and yidams should only be done after realization of shunyata.

TRUNGPA RINPOCHE: I wouldn't say complete realization,

but the person should have practice in shunyata first, know how to perceive the world on the shunyata level first.

S: It seems to me that other Tibetan teachers give visualization practices to new students. Why would they do that?

TR: In Tibet, most serious practitioners would automatically enter vajrayana immediately. But theoretically they already have some training in the basic practice of meditation. A lot of Western students come to teachers in what is seemingly the same faithful, devoted fashion as Tibetans, but they have no training behind them. So it seems to be premature to start them with vajrayana practices, when they have not even realized the meaning of suffering or of the four noble truths. They can't just start with visualization.

There is another problem with Western practitioners. Whether they consider themselves Christians or followers of the theistic tradition or not, still their general thinking pattern, their fundamental way of carrying their mind about in this world on the spiritual level, is still based on the theistic tradition. A lot of people may have reservations about believing in an external god and things like that, but still their basic approach goes along with a theistic attitude. Then if they visualize another god, that doesn't sort anything out for them at all. It just reinforces their national ego or religious ego, which they immediately associate with this. Somehow it just becomes an extra burden rather than an approach toward freedom.

STUDENT: Isn't it what you call "idiot compassion" to start students with vajrayana practices? It seems to make so much more sense to begin with the hinayana and mahayana approach of moment-to-moment compassion toward your own mind.

TRUNGPA RINPOCHE: I think so, yes. Generally, I think we have a kind of social problem here. When Western students come to study with Eastern teachers, they are regarded as special guests, because they come from the land that invented airplanes, motorcars, radios, and other fantastic things of all kinds. There is already something special about them; they have their passport by birth. This is particularly true for Tibetans, for instance. In Tibetan, the word for "foreigner" is not at all derogatory. It has a sense of the exotic. Foreigners are not regarded as barbarians at all, but are thought to be very smart and have powerful minds. As a Tibetan, you might think that one American visitor in your monastery could build airplanes for you if you wanted, or motorcars, fountains, electric plants, or anything. Westerners are considered all-knowing, omniscient. Although they may not actually have any knowledge at all, because of that kind of credentials, they are put in the category of special guests, which is actually quite close to idiot compassion. The hard-core ego or neurosis they in fact carry calls for much more training.

STUDENT: There are literally thousands of people in the West practicing hatha yoga. Are these people making a mistake? Are they not prepared for hatha yoga?

TRUNGPA RINPOCHE: If you relate with hatha yoga on a hinayana level, like instead of just sitting cross-legged and meditating, then it seems to be okay. A lot of people approach it as just a gymnastic thing. But if they begin to play with psychophysical energy with a semitantric approach, as in kundalini yoga, for instance, then it tends to become very dangerous.

STUDENT: I don't understand what you said about miracles. It seems to me that even if you were thrown into jail for producing money out of thin air, it would still be a miracle.

TRUNGPA RINPOCHE: It would be criminal. You are not

helping the karma of the country. You are creating more unemployment and more pain, which cheapens the energy, green energy.[2] Producing money is an insult to the mandala.

STUDENT: Is the idea of the dream yoga to realize how completely the world you perceive is made out of your own projections? Is it that once you realize that and relate to it enough, you're really being more realistic?

TRUNGPA RINPOCHE: That's right, yes.

STUDENT: What do you mean by a *real* dream state?

TRUNGPA RINPOCHE: This, the way we are now. You are asleep.

STUDENT: What form does the intelligence that develops into mahamudra take at the hinayana and mahayana levels?

TRUNGPA RINPOCHE: The hinayana level of intelligence is mindfulness. I suppose we could say that the prajna level that comes then is awareness, which is greater than just being mindful of particular things. Mindfulness is also very intelligent, but that intelligence is not as great as awareness. Mindfulness is sometimes called "recollection" (*smriti* in Sanskrit), which does not mean recollecting the past, but recollecting what is happening here now. In the actual, real, final prajna, awareness becomes all-pervasive. You don't have to project in any particular direction or from any particular angle. It is everywhere. But still there is a sense of pulsation, of flash and spread, flash and spread. It isn't a constant thing.

S: What changes that causes the mindfulness to progress to awareness?

TR: Awareness develops because mindfulness begins to see things so precisely and clearly that the things begin to put out radiations of awareness, rather than just being the object you're being mindful of. That permeates. It is an opening. For instance, if you look at a candle, you begin to see not only the candle but also the light that candle is reflecting at other objects. Your vision becomes much greater. That brings intelligence into another area. Awareness is not only awareness of things, but also awareness of space everywhere. You cannot develop such awareness without first developing mindfulness of things.

STUDENT: Are the six dharmas of Naropa meditation practices?

TRUNGPA RINPOCHE: They are a kind of meditation practice, I suppose you could say, but they have more to do with relating with the activity of your life; they are more on the level of meditation in action. Of course there are certain techniques for developing the six dharmas, different tricks, so to speak, visualizations and mantras and so on. But the general idea is that you do those as a preparation, and the actual practice happens in your everyday life situation.

STUDENT: You described various views of sacredness. It seemed on the whole that one had to do with God and the other one was the vajrayana approach. I was wondering whether one of these applied to the mahayana idea of sacredness, or if that was still another outlook. It seems to me that traditionally there's such a strong element of devotion and sacred richness in it that mahayana almost sounds like Catholicism.

TRUNGPA RINPOCHE: I think the mahayana is much closer to the theistic approach, definitely, because it has a sense of greatness and it emphasizes performing transcending actions—which is still related with size. The vajrayana no longer relates to size; it relates to qualities. The mahayana is the "big vehicle." The vajrayana is the "diamond vehicle"; it could be big or small.

S: There's something confusing about the emphasis on grandioseness in the mahayana, since it's essential teaching is shunyata. I would have thought shunyata would cut through the grandioseness as pretentious.

TR: Well, it should cut, but somehow it doesn't entirely. Therefore mahayana can lead into vajrayana. It's not so much that the grandioseness is cut down, but the grandioseness doesn't exist, so the whole setup begins to fall apart. That's the trick. This particularly happens in the later stages of the mahayana, like the eighth, ninth, and tenth bhumis. Definitely by the tenth bhumi there is no viewer anymore.

S: And the grandioseness—

TR: Just dissolves into dharmakaya. Like a car without a driver goes to the dump.

STUDENT: Do you have to be a trickster to get enlightened? It seems there are a lot of tricks involved.

TRUNGPA RINPOCHE: I should say so, yes.

STUDENT: At this vajrayana level, where do reference points come in, if they come in at all?

TRUNGPA RINPOCHE: The energies. In vajrayana, the reference point is not regarded as bad, but it is the way of accentuating the play of phenomena.

STUDENT: But is there a reference point?

TRUNGPA RINPOCHE: There is a vajra reference point rather than an ordinary reference point, which is wisdom.

STUDENT: Why would you accentuate the play of the ordinary?

TRUNGPA RINPOCHE: You are not doing it. Phenomena as they are accentuate themselves.

S: I see.

TR: That's it!

STUDENT: How does the idea of a person having an aim fit in, or is that gone by this time?

TRUNGPA RINPOCHE: An ordinary student might still have a sense of struggle, but in moments when flashes take place, when realizations take place in his state of mind, there's no aim. You remember the idea of ordinary mind we were talking about? The ordinariness? That's it.

STUDENT: It's almost as if you and energy or you and the universe, or whatever you want to call it, are the same.

TRUNGPA RINPOCHE: It's very simple. It's so simple. And there's a sense of well-being, so no ambition is involved, except entertaining oneself constantly—which the entertainments do for you, rather than your having to order them.

STUDENT: And compassion kind of comes in naturally.

TRUNGPA RINPOCHE: Yes. When you're lighting incense in your room, which clears the air, that's the compassion. It makes things workable, pleasant to be.

STUDENT: Why is the illusory body called illusory body?

TRUNGPA RINPOCHE: It's the same idea as the dream. This is a dream.

S: Oh, maybe I didn't understand right. I thought if one realized the illusory body, that was being more real.

TR: That's what I mean. It's the same as the dream. This is a dream, which is real. More real than the ordinary sleeping dream, than the dream dream.

S: This is a real dream.

TR: Yes, this is a real dream.

S: That means there is reality.

TR: There is reality, sure. And there is unreality at the same time.

S: The unreality is the dream.

TR: Is *not* the dream. The real dream is reality. And the real illusion is the real thing. In other words, the mirage is the real water. You know, when you see a mirage in the desert—a lake with palm trees? That's real. You may not find it when you get there, when you want to have a drink of water, but still it's real.

S: If you're in the desert, though, you have to distinguish between the real oasis and the fake one.

TR: That's what I mean. That's what I mean, yes.

STUDENT: How does the realization of the illusory body connect with that?

TRUNGPA RINPOCHE: You are able to see real things, things that shimmer, change energy, shift patterns.

S: Like a mirage?

TR: Like a mirage; like you and I looking at each other now. That's the real illusory body. I change and you change, this way and that way. But it's a real change.

S: Then an unreal change would be if you were hallucinating.

TR: Yes.

STUDENT: Could you say that real doesn't apply to anything particular, but we're just talking about clearing perception?

TRUNGPA RINPOCHE: Clearing perception, yes. It's catching yourself, fragments of yourself, assembling this particular perception. That's the illusory body.

S: Learning how to spot that.

TR: Learning how to spot that, yes.

S: How to spot that detail and even make use of it?

TR: Yes.

S: And still keep track of it as an illusion.

TR: Yes. And very sanely.

S: So actually it's a very real energy.

TR: You've got it, . . . I think.

STUDENT: Are you saying there's a message involved in your perception at that point?

TRUNGPA RINPOCHE: Not really messages. That's secondary. Third-hand. But this is *first*-hand. Even zero-hand.

STUDENT: I still don't understand the relationship between the mirage and the reality.

TRUNGPA RINPOCHE: The mirage *is* reality. It's a real mirage.

S: There's no fake mirage, then.

TR: No. It's very real.

S: That doesn't quite accord with my understanding of mirage, or at least what I was taught at school.

TR: What did they say?

S: A mirage is something you think is there and it's not.

TR: Well, that's it!

S: That's reality?

TR: That's reality.

S: So if I see a mirage, say of an oasis, the mirage is real, but the water, the palm trees, and the coconuts are not real.

TR: That's right, yes. I think you've got it.

S: Is a memory a mirage in that sense?

TR: Yes, precisely. That's a good question.

STUDENT: Are you saying that to see the mirage as a mirage is to see reality?

TRUNGPA RINPOCHE: That's the first thing. There is a song about that in the book, actually. It's in the section about Marpa meeting Naropa. Could somebody read that?

STUDENT [reads poem from p. 101]:

> The sky-flower, the Daka riding on the foal
> Of a barren mare, the Oral Transmission,
> Has scattered the hairs of a tortoise, the ineffable,
> And with the poke of a hare's horn, the
>   unoriginated,
> Roused Tilopa in the depth of ultimate reality.
>
> Through the mute Tilopa, the ineffable resisting
>   all attempts at communication,
> The blind Naropa became free in seeing Truth
>   which is no seeing.
> On the mountain of the Dharmakaya which is the
>   ultimate, the deaf Naropa,
> The lame Mati (Mar-pa) ran in a radiant light,
>   which neither comes nor goes.
> The sun and moon and dGyes-pa rdor-rje—
> Their dancing is one-valueness in many.

The conch-shell has proclaimed its fame in all
       directions,
It has called out to the strenuous, who are worthy
       vessels for instruction.
The focal points, Chakrasamvara—the world
Is the wheel of the Oral Transmission:
Turn it, dear child, without attachment.

TRUNGPA RINPOCHE: We should end our seminar here. I think you should read this song again and again if you can. It makes enormous sense. The translation is the best we have so far, and Dr. Guenther's very genuine effort has become a very valuable medium. He doesn't try to put in his own ideas. He tries to present the translation directly, as it is, which lays very important groundwork for us. Obviously, we have to discuss more about mahamudra and this mirage and so forth.

Notes

PART ONE

Chapter 1.   Naropa and Us

1. Abhayakirti (Tib. 'Jig-med grags-pa), according to Guenther, "was the name which Naropa had when he renounced his post of abbot at Nalanda and set out in search of his Guru." Literally the name means "renowned as fearless."

Chapter 2.   Genuine Madness and Pop Art

1. *Ku-su-li-pa* is a Tibetan term, often also appearing as *kusulu,* describing a yogi who has reached such a level of simplicity that he only has thoughts concerning three things: eating, sleeping, and eliminating.

2. "*Lohivagaja* seems to be the Tibetan transcription of a Prakrit sentence which in Sanskrit might have been *rohita avagaccha,* 'fish go away!' " (Guenther's note, *The Life and Teaching of Naropa,* p. 35).

3. G. I. Gurdjieff was a well-known teacher of Greek-Armenian origin who taught his own system of spirituality in eastern and western Europe and the United States in the first half of the twentieth century. The Vidyadhara adopted Gurdjieff's notion of "idiot compassion," a "feel-good" approach of seeming kindness that actually contributes further to delusion and weakness.

PART 2

Chapter 2. Giving Birth to Intellect

1. Don Juan is the sorcerer and spiritual teacher of the Yaqui Indian tribe of northern Mexico described in the many books of Carlos Castaneda.

Chapter 4. Beyond Shunyata

1. "Emptiness being form": This is a reference to the *Heart Sutra*, or *Sutra of the Heart of Transcendent Knowledge* (Skt. *Mahaprajnaparamitahridaya-sutra*). A key line in this sutra is "Form is no other than emptiness; emptiness is no other than form." This line is sometimes interpreted, as by the questioner here, as indicating two stages in the understanding of shunyata, or emptiness. In the first, the practitioner realizes that forms have no essence that makes them ultimately real and thus are "empty." This understanding may be associated with a tendency to reject or withdraw from the world. In a further stage, the practitioner realizes that it is the nature of emptiness to appear as forms. This may prompt the fully realized person's return to the world. This analysis of shunyata is particularly stressed in Zen.

Chapter 6. The Levels of Mahamudra

1. "The last one has to do with sleep": The six dharmas of Naropa are usually listed as: (1) inner heat (Tib. *tumo*), (2) illusory body (*gyulü*), (3) dream (*milam*), (4) luminosity (*ösel*), (5) transference (*phowa*), (6) bardo, or in-between state. Though these may be given in a different order, the editor has no explanation for why the Vidyadhara chose to expound the last one as he does here.

2. "Green energy": Playing on the color of American bank notes, the Vidyadhara sometimes half-jocularly referred to money as green energy.

Glossary

THE DEFINITIONS GIVEN in this glossary are particular to their usage in this book and should not be construed as the single or even most common meaning of a specific term. Unless otherwise designated, foreign terms in the glossary are Sanskrit.

abhisheka   "Anointment." A ceremony in which a student is ritually introduced into a mandala of a particular tantric deity by a tantric master and is thus empowered to visualize and invoke that particular deity. The essential element of abhisheka is a meeting of minds between master and student.

Adhidhana-uttaratantra   The root tantra of the male yidam Chakrasamvara.

arhat   A "worthy one," who has attained the highest level of hinayana.

ati   "Great perfection." The primary teaching of the Nyingma school of Tibetan Buddhism. This teaching is considered the final statement of the fruition path of vajrayana. It is called "great" because there is nothing more sublime; it is called "perfection" because no further means are necessary. According to the experience of ati practitioners, purity of mind is always present and needs only to be recognized.

Atisha Dipankara (980/90–1055)   A Buddhist scholar of royal family who particularly systematized the method for generating enlightened mind.

bhikshu   Beggar; monk; male member of the Buddhist sangha who has entered homelessness and received full ordination.

bhumi   "Land." Each of the ten stages that a bodhisattva must go through to attain buddhahood: (1) very joyful, (2) stainless, (3) luminous, (4) radiant, (5) difficult to conquer, (6) face-to-face, (7) far-going, (8) immovable, (9) having good intellect, and (10) cloud of dharma.

bodhisattva   "Awake being." Someone who has completely overcome confusion and dedicated his or her life and all his or her actions to awakening or liberating all sentient beings.

bodhisattva path   Another name for the mahayana.

buddhadharma   The Buddha's teaching; Buddhism.

buddha families   The mandala of the five buddha families represents five basic styles of energy, which could manifest dualistically as confusion or nondualistically as enlightenment. The enlightened mandala is portrayed iconographically as the mandala of the five *tathagatas,* or victorious ones. All experience is said to be colored by one of these five energies. The central, or buddha, family represents ignorance which can be transformed into the wisdom of all-encompassing space. In the east is the vajra family, representing aggression, which can be transformed into mirror-like wisdom. In the south is the ratna family, representing pride, which can be transformed into the wisdom of equanimity. In the west is the padma family of passion, which can be transformed into discriminating awareness wisdom. And in the north is the karma family of envy, which can be transformed into the wisdom that accomplishes all action.

buddha nature According to the mahayana view, the true, immutable, and eternal nature of all beings. Since all beings possess this buddha nature, it is possible for them to attain enlightenment and become a buddha, regardless of what level of existence they occupy.

buddha principles *See* buddha families.

daka Specifically, a masculine semiwrathful yidam. More generally, it can refer to a type of messenger or protector.

dharmakaya One of the three bodies of buddhahood. The dharmakaya is enlightenment itself, wisdom beyond any reference point—unoriginated primordial mind, devoid of content.

duhkha "Suffering." *Duhkha satya,* "the truth of suffering," is the first of Buddha's four noble truths. The term refers to physical and psychological suffering of all kinds, including the subtle but all-pervading frustration we experience with regard to the impermanence and insubstantiality of all things.

hinayana The "lesser vehicle," in which the practitioner concentrates on basic meditation practice and an understanding of basic Buddhist doctrines such as the four noble truths.

jnana The wisdom-activity of enlightenment, transcending all dualistic conceptualization.

Kagyupa (Tib.) "Command lineage." One of the four principal schools of Tibetan Buddhism. The Kagyu lineage is known as the Practice Lineage because of its emphasis on meditative discipline.

karmamudra   A tantric practice utilizing a consort.

mahamudra   "Great seal, symbol, or gesture." The central meditative transmission of the Kagyu lineage. The inherent clarity and wakefulness of mind, which is both vivid and empty.

mahayana   The "greater vehicle," which emphasizes the emptiness (shunyata) of all phenomena, compassion, and the acknowledgment of universal buddha nature. The ideal figure of the mahayana is the bodhisattva; hence it is often referred to as the bodhisattva path.

mandala   A total vision that unifies the seeming complexity and chaos of experience into a simple pattern and natural hierarchy. The Tibetan word *khyilkhor* used to translate the Sanskrit term literally means "center and surroundings." A mandala is usually represented two-dimensionally as a four-sided diagram with a central deity, a personification of the basic sanity of buddha nature. Three-dimensionally, it is a palace with a center and four gates in the cardinal directions.

Manjushri   "He Who Is Noble and Gentle." The bodhisattva of knowledge and learning. Usually depicted with a book and the sword of prajna.

mantra   Mantras are Sanskrit words or syllables that are recited ritually as the quintessence of various energies. For instance, they can be used to attract particular energies or to repel obstructions.

mindfulness   Practicing mindfulness in Buddhism means to perform consciously all activities, including everyday, automatic activities such as breathing and walking, and to assume the attitude of "pure observation," through which clear knowledge, i.e., clearly conscious thinking and acting, is attained. The intention of mindfulness practice is to bring the mind under control and to a state of rest.

Nagarjuna (second/third century) A great Indian teacher of Buddhism, the founder of the Madhyamaka school of Buddhist philosophy. He contributed greatly to the logical development of the doctrine of shunyata and was the author of many key texts as well as, in legend, the guru of various important Buddhist teachers who lived centuries apart.

nirmanakaya "Emanation body," "form body," or "body of manifestation." Communication of awakened mind through form—specifically, through embodiment as a human being.

nirvana The idea of enlightenment according to the hinayana. It is the cessation of ignorance and conflicting emotions and therefore freedom from compulsive rebirth in samsara.

pandit "Scholar." A scholar or learned person who studies and interprets sacred texts as an intellectual activity.

paramita "That which has reached the other shore." The six paramitas, or "perfections," are generosity, discipline, patience, exertion, meditation, and knowledge.

prajna "Transcendental knowledge." Prajna, the sixth paramita, is called transcendental because it sees through the veils of dualistic confusion.

pranayama A form of yoga practiced in the vajrayana, which involves working with the illusory body by means of controlling mind, breath, and body.

Rangjung Dorje (1284–1339) The third Karmapa, spiritual leader of the Karma Kagyu lineage.

Rudra   Originally a Hindu deity, an emanation of Shiva. In the vajrayana, Rudra is the personification of the destructive principle of ultimate ego. Traditionally, Rudra was a student who perverted the teachings, eventually killing his guru. Rudrahood is the complete opposite of buddhahood.

sadhana   A ritual text, as well as the accompanying practice. Ranging from very simple to more elaborate versions, sadhanas engage the mind through meditation, the body through gestures *(mudras)*, and the speech through mantra recitation.

samaya   "Coming together." The vajrayana principle of commitment, whereby the student is bound completely to the discipline and to the teacher and to his or her own sanity.

sambhogakaya   "Enjoyment body." The environment of compassion and communication linking the dharmakaya and the nirmanakaya.

samsara   "Journeying." The vicious cycle of transmigratory existence. It arises out of ignorance and is characterized by suffering.

Saraha   An Indian teacher referred to in Tibetan texts as "Great Brahmin." Tradition has it that he was born 336 years after the Buddha's death, and that he was the spiritual master of Nagarjuna.

shunyata   "Emptiness, void." A completely open and unbounded clarity of mind.

siddha   "Perfect, complete." One who possesses *siddhis,* or "perfect abilities." There are eight ordinary siddhis: indomitability, the ability to see the gods, fleetness of foot, invisibility, longevity, the ability to fly, the ability to make certain medicines, and power over the world of spirits and demons. The single "supreme" siddhi is enlightenment.

skandha   "Group, aggregate, heap." Each of the five aggregates, which constitute the entirety of what is generally known as "personality." They are form, sensation, perception, mental formations, and consciousness. These are frequently referred to as "aggregates of attachment," since (except in the case of arhats and buddhas) craving or desire attaches itself to them and attracts them to itself; thus it makes of them objects of attachment and brings about suffering.

skillful means   *See* upaya.

spiritual materialism   "Walking the spiritual path properly is a very subtle process; it is not something to jump into naively. There are numerous sidetracks which lead to a distorted, ego-centered version of spirituality; we can deceive ourselves into thinking we are developing spiritually when instead we are strengthening our egocentricity through spiritual techniques. This fundamental distortion may be referred to as *spiritual materialism*."—Chögyam Trungpa

tantra   A synonym for vajrayana, the third of the three yanas of Tibetan Buddhism. *Tantra* means continuity and refers both to the root texts of the vajrayana and to the systems of meditation they describe.

trikaya   "Three bodies." The three bodies of buddhahood. The dharmakaya is enlightenment itself, wisdom beyond any reference point—unoriginated primordial mind, devoid of content. The sambhogakaya is the environment of compassion and communication. The nirmanakaya is the buddha that actually takes form as a human, who eats, sleeps, and shares his life with his students.

Tripitaka   "Three Baskets." The canon of Buddhist scriptures, consisting of three parts: the Vinaya-pitaka, the

Sutra-pitaka, and the Abhidharma-pitaka. The first "basket" contains accounts of the origins of the Buddhist community (sangha) as well as the rules of discipline regulating the lives of monks and nuns. The second is composed of discourse said to have come from the mouth of the Buddha or his immediate disciples. The third part is a compendium of Buddhist psychology and philosophy.

upaya   Skill in means or method. 1. The ability of a bodhisattva to guide beings to liberation through skillful means. All possible methods and ruses from straightforward talk to the most conspicuous miracles could be applicable. 2. Skill in expounding the teaching.

vajrayana   "Diamond vehicle." The third of the three main yanas of Tibetan Buddhism. Vajrayana is also known as the sudden path, because it is claimed that through the practice of vajrayana one can realize enlightenment in one lifetime.

Vajrayogini   A semiwrathful yidam. She is red, with one face and two arms, young and beautiful, but enraged and wearing ornaments of human bones. She represents the transformation of ignorance and passion into shunyata and compassion.

vihara   "Sojourning place." A residence for monks, to which they can also retire for meditation.

vipashyana   "Insight" or "clear seeing." With *shamatha* ("tranquillity"), one of the two main modes of meditation common to all forms of Buddhism.

yana   "Vehicle." A coherent body of intellectual teachings and practical meditative methods related to a particular stage of a student's progress on the path of buddhadharma.

The three main vehicles are the hinayana, mahayana, and vajrayana. These can also be subdivided to make nine yanas.

yidam (Tib.) "Firm mind." The vajrayana practitioner's personal deity, who embodies the practitioner's awakened nature. Yidams are usually sambhogakaya buddhas.

Transliterations of Tibetan Terms

bardo	*bar do*
gyulü	*sgyu lus*
gyuwa	*rgyu ba*
khyilkhor	*dkyil 'khor*
milam	*rmi lam*
naro chödruk	*naro chos drug*
ösel	*'od gsal*
phowa	*'pho ba*
tumo	*gtum mo*
yidam	*yi dam*

About the Author

VEN. CHÖGYAM TRUNGPA was born in the province of Kham in Eastern Tibet in 1940. When he was just thirteen months old, Chögyam Trungpa was recognized as a major *tülku,* or incarnate teacher. According to Tibetan tradition, an enlightened teacher is capable, based on his or her vow of compassion, of reincarnating in human form over a succession of generations. Before dying, such a teacher leaves a letter or other clues to the whereabouts of the next incarnation. Later, students and other realized teachers look through these clues and, based on careful examination of dreams and visions, conduct searches to discover and recognize the successor. Thus, particular lines of teaching are formed, in some cases extending over several centuries. Chögyam Trungpa was the eleventh in the teaching lineage known as the Trungpa Tülkus.

Once young tülkus are recognized, they enter a period of intensive training in the theory and practice of the Buddhist teachings. Trungpa Rinpoche (*Rinpoche* is an honorific title meaning "precious one"), after being enthroned as supreme abbot of Surmang monastery and governor of Surmang District, began a period of training that would last eighteen years, until his departure from Tibet in 1959. As a Kagyü tülku, his training was based on the systematic practice of meditation and on refined theoretical understanding of Buddhist philosophy. One of the four great lineages of Tibet, the Kagyü is known as the "practice lineage."

At the age of eight, Trungpa Rinpoche received ordination as a novice monk. After his ordination, he engaged in intensive study and practice of the traditional monastic disciplines as well as in the arts of calligraphy, thangka painting, and monastic dance. His primary teachers were Jamgön Kongtrül of Sechen and Khenpo Kangshar—leading teachers in the Nyingma and Kagyü lineages. In 1958, at the age of eighteen, Trungpa Rinpoche completed his studies, receiving the degrees of *kyorpön* (doctor of divinity) and *khenpo* (master of studies). He also received full monastic ordination.

The late fifties were a time of great upheaval in Tibet. As it became clear that the Chinese Communists intended to take over the country by force, many people, both monastic and lay, fled the country. Trungpa Rinpoche spent many harrowing months trekking over the Himalayas (described in his book *Born in Tibet*). After narrowly escaping capture by the Chinese, he at last reached India in 1959. While in India, Trungpa Rinpoche was appointed to serve as spiritual adviser to the Young Lamas Home School in Dalhousie, India. He served in this capacity from 1959 to 1963.

Trungpa Rinpoche's first opportunity to encounter the West came when he received a Spaulding sponsorship to attend Oxford University. At Oxford he studied comparative religion, philosophy, and fine arts. He also studied Japanese flower arranging, receiving a degree from the Sogetsu School. While in England, Trungpa Rinpoche began to instruct Western students in the dharma (the teachings of the Buddha), and in 1968 he cofounded the Samye Ling Meditation Centre in Dumfriesshire, Scotland. During this period he also published his first two books, both in English: *Born in Tibet* and *Meditation in Action*.

In 1969, Trungpa Rinpoche traveled to Bhutan, where he entered into a solitary meditation retreat. This retreat marked a pivotal change in his approach to teaching. Immediately upon returning he became a lay person, putting aside his monastic robes and dressing in ordinary Western attire. He also married a young Englishwoman, and together they left Scotland and moved to North America. Many of his early students found these changes shocking and upsetting. However, he expressed a conviction that, in order to take root in the West, the dharma needed to be taught free from cultural trappings and religious fascination.

During the seventies America was in a period of political and cultural ferment. It was a time of fascination with the East. Trungpa Rinpoche criticized the materialistic and commercialized approach to spirituality he encountered, describing it as a "spiritual supermarket." In his lectures, and in his books *Cutting Through Spiritual Materialism* and *The Myth of Freedom,* he pointed to the simplicity and directness of the practice of sitting meditation as the way to cut through such distortions of the spiritual journey.

During his seventeen years of teaching in North America, Trungpa Rinpoche developed a reputation as a dynamic and controversial teacher. Fluent in the English language, he was one of the first lamas who could speak to Western students directly, without the aid of a translator. Traveling extensively throughout North America and Europe, Trungpa Rinpoche gave hundreds of talks and seminars. He established major centers in Vermont, Colorado, and Nova Scotia, as well as many smaller meditation and study centers in cities throughout North America and Europe. Vajradhatu was formed in 1973 as the central administrative body of this network.

In 1974, Trungpa Rinpoche founded the Naropa Institute,

which became the only accredited Buddhist-inspired university in North America. He lectured extensively at the Institute, and his book *Journey without Goal* is based on a course he taught there. In 1976, he established the Shambhala Training program, a series of weekend programs and seminars that provides instruction in meditation practice within a secular setting. His book *Shambhala: The Sacred Path of the Warrior* gives an overview of the Shambhala teachings.

In 1976, Trungpa Rinpoche appointed Ösel Tendzin (Thomas F. Rich) as his Vajra Regent, or dharma heir. Ösel Tendzin worked closely with Trungpa Rinpoche in the administration of Vajradhatu and Shambhala Training. He taught extensively from 1976 until his death in 1990 and is the author of *Buddha in the Palm of Your Hand.*

Trungpa Rinpoche was also active in the field of translation. Working with Francesca Fremantle, he rendered a new translation of *The Tibetan Book of the Dead,* which was published in 1975. Later he formed the Nalanda Translation Committee, in order to translate texts and liturgies for his own students as well as to make important texts available publicly.

In 1978 Trungpa Rinpoche conducted a ceremony empowering his son Ösel Rangdröl Mukpo as his successor in the Shambhala lineage. At that time he gave him the title of Sawang, or "earth lord."

Trungpa Rinpoche was also known for his interest in the arts and particularly for his insights into the relationship between contemplative discipline and the artistic process. His own art work included calligraphy, painting, flower arranging, poetry, playwriting, and environmental installations. In addition, at the Naropa Institute he created an educational atmosphere that attracted many leading artists and poets. The exploration of the creative process in light of contemplative training continues there as a provocative dialogue. Trungpa

Rinpoche also published two books of poetry: *Mudra* and *First Thought Best Thought*.

Trungpa Rinpoche's published books represent only a fraction of the rich legacy of his teachings. During his seventeen years of teaching in North America, he crafted the structures necessary to provide his students with thorough, systematic training in the dharma. From introductory talks and courses to advanced group retreat practices, these programs emphasize a balance of study and practice, of intellect and intuition. Students at all levels can pursue their interest in meditation and the Buddhist path through these many forms of training. Senior students of Trungpa Rinpoche continue to be involved in both teaching and meditation instruction in such programs. In addition to his extensive teachings in the Buddhist tradition, Trungpa Rinpoche also placed great emphasis on the Shambhala teachings, which stress the importance of mind-training, as distinct from religious practice; community involvement and the creation of an enlightened society; and appreciation of one's day-to-day life.

Trungpa Rinpoche passed away in 1987, at the age of forty-seven. He is survived by his wife, Diana, and five sons. His eldest son, the Sawang Ösel Rangdröl Mukpo, succeeds him as president and spiritual head of Vajradhatu. By the time of his death, Trungpa Rinpoche had become known as a pivotal figure in introducing dharma to the Western world. The joining of his great appreciation for Western culture and his deep understanding of his own tradition led to a revolutionary approach to teaching the dharma, in which the most ancient and profound teachings were presented in a thoroughly contemporary way. Trungpa Rinpoche was known for his fearless proclamation of the dharma: free from hesitation, true to the purity of the tradition, and utterly fresh. May these teachings take root and flourish for the benefit of all sentient beings.

Meditation Center Information

FOR FURTHER INFORMATION regarding meditation or inquiries about a dharma center near you, please contact one of the following centers.

Karmê-Chöling
Star Route
Barnet, VT 05821
(802) 633-2384

Rocky Mountain Dharma Center
4921 County Road 68C
Red Feather Lakes, CO 80545
(303) 881-2184

Vajradhatu Europe
Zwetchenweg 23
D3550 Marburg
Germany
49 6421 34244

Vajradhatu International
1084 Tower Road
Halifax, N.S. B3H 2Y5
Canada
(902) 425-4275

Many talks and seminars are available in cassette tape format. For information, call or write:

Vajradhatu Recordings
1084 Tower Road
Halifax, N.S. B3H 2Y5
Canada
(902) 421-1550

For information about Buddhist postsecondary education, call or write:

The Naropa Institute
2130 Arapahoe Ave.
Boulder, CO 80302
(303) 444-0202

Index

Abhayakirti, 5, 151n.1–1
  See also Naropa
Abhisheka ("initiation"), 131
Aggression, 69–70, 85
  as energy, 95
Aloneness
  satori and, 94
  shunyata and, 93
Analytical mind, 75–77
Anger, 85–86
  psychosomatic tension and,
    136–137
Appreciation, 47–48
Arhat(s), 55–56, 77
  egolessness and, 98–99
Art
  pop, 17
  Tibetan Buddhist, 17
Awareness, 124, 135–136
  choiceless (shunyata), 89–99
  discriminating, 73
  mindfulness and, 143–144
  prajna and, 72
  vs. wakefulness, 139

Bardo doctrine, 50–51
Basic sanity, 131

Black magic, 27–28
Bliss, 19, 120–121
  irritation and, 129
  pain and, 19
  pleasure as, 121
Bodhisattva(s), 77–78
  as princes, 83
  seventh bhumi, 77
  sixth bhumi, 95, 114–115
  tenth bhumi, 145
Bodhisattva path, 127
  skillful means and, 131
Body, 41–42, 136–138
  ego and, 42, 43
  hatha yoga and, 139
  illusory, 137, 147–148
  mind-body, 36
  phowa and, 138
  reality and, 47
  tumo and, 136–137
Buddha(s)
  American, 25
  as kings, 83
  prajna as mother of, 89
  principles, five, 131, 135
  three types of, 55
Buddha nature, 96

Buddhism
  hinayana, 30, 55–56, 98
  mahayana, 30, 55, 122, 144–145
  Tibetan, 17
  vajrayana, 55, 56, 122, 124, 127–
    134, 140–141, 145–146
  Zen, 94, 152n.4–1

Chandali. *See* Inner heat
Christianity, 2
Clarity, 87
  as confidence/fearlessness, 131
  Don Juan on, 82
  mahamudra as, 116, 131, 134
Coemergent wisdom, 118
Communication, 89
Compassion, 21, 84, 146
  absolute, 29–30
  as bad medicine for ego, 29
  idiot, 29–30, 37, 151n.2–3
  prajna and, 82
  shunyata and, 89, 96
  three yanas and, 30
  as trust in oneself, 82
  tumo and, 136
Concept(s), 6–7, 16
Confidence, 91
  five buddha principles and, 131,
    135
Conflicting emotions, 38
Confusion, 3–4, 16, 22, 28, 32, 108–
    109, 110, 113
  coemergent wisdom and, 118, 127
  as ground, 112
  hopelessness and, 63
  Naropa's, as ours, 19–20, 108
  prajna and, 100
  precision and, 19
  shunyata and, 100
Continuity, 98
  definition of tantra, 56, 64
  discontinuity as, 64

of ego, 27, 64
of three-yanas, 116
Crazy wisdom, 120

Deities, 132
  sense perceptions and, 135
  yidam principle and, 134
Devil(s), 27–28
Dharmakaya, 55
Discipline, 98
  samaya, 107
Discriminating awareness, 73
Disneyland quality of life, 137–138
Don Juan, 82, 152n.2–1
Dream yoga (Tib. *milam*), 50, 137–
    138, 143
Dreams/fantasies, 50, 143, 146–147
  as dharma, 137–138
  vs. reality, 32–33, 46–48
Duality, 28–29, 74
  subject/object, 88
  See also Nonduality

Ego, 64, 83–85, 98
  duality and, 88
  emotions and, 38–39
  exposing, 58–60
  as fuel, 43–44
  killing of, 21–22, 29
  madness and, 23
  mahamudra experience and,
    125–126
  pain and, 57–58
  pleasure and, 120–121
  shunyata and, 126
  shyness of, 86
  spiritual materialism and, 28
  symbolism of, 42
  theism and, 141
  watcher and, 27
Egolessness, 88
  arhat experience of, 98–99

continuity of, 64
  pain and, 126
Elements (physical/psychological), 140
Emotion(s)
  conflicting, 38
  ego and, 38–39
  prajna and, 76–78, 79–81
  resentment and, 85–86
  stages of, 42–43
Emptiness, 90
  form and, 152n.4–1
  fullness and, 93
  mahamudra and, 116–117
Energy, 82, 95
Enlightenment, 26, 131
  confusion and, 3, 16
  continuity of, 64
  killing of ego and, 21–22
  samsara and, 44
  three levels of, 55
  trickery and, 145
Expectation, 37–38
Experience as process, 91

Fascination
  vs. appreciation, 47–48
  emotions and, 39
  with pain, 64
  symbolism and, 26–27
Fearlessness, 124, 131
  seeing/looking and, 78
Feminine principle, 89
Five buddha principles, 131

Gap, 48
Giving up
  beliefs (inner phenomena), 38
  hope, 32–33
God. *See* Theism
Good/evil, 27–28
  watcher and, 29
Green energy, 143, 152n.6–2

Groundlessness, 88, 89, 124
  mahamudra and, 116
  ordinariness and, 92–93
Guenther, Herbert V., 150
Gurdjieff, G. I., 29, 151n.2–3
Guru, 4, 97
  Naropa's search for, 8–20, 32, 41.
    See also Twelve trials of Naropa
  as pill/seed in you, 128–130
  role of, 65
  See also Vajra master

Hallucinogenic experience, 127
Hatha yoga
  hinayana level, 142
  vajrayana level, 139–140, 142
Hinayana, 30, 55–56
  shunyata experience, 98
  teacher, 122
Hope
  and fear, 60–61
  giving up, 32–33
  pain and, 55–69
  spiritual materialism, 61–62
Hopelessness, 55–69
  as remedy, 63
  as requirement for spiritual path,
    61, 62
  well-being and, 67
Humpty Dumpty, 58

Identifying with teachings, 93, 94, 97
Idiot compassion, 29–30, 141–142,
    151n.2–3
  reality vs., 37
Ignorance, 102, 106–109
Illusory body (Tib. *gyulü*), 50, 137,
    147–148
  perception and, 148
Impermanence, 98
Impressions/expressions, 136
Inner heat (Tib. *tumo*), 51, 136–137
  compassion and, 136

Inquisitiveness, 62
Insanity/sanity, 16–17, 22–23, 27
   hopelessness and, 63
Intellect (Skt. *prajna*)
   birth of, 69–88
   irritations and, 80–81, 85
   pain and, 70–71
   See also Prajna
Intellect/intuition, 56, 68
Intelligence
   hinayana, 143
   mahayana, 143
   mantra and, 56–57
   pain and, 56, 63
   resentment and, 84
   tantric insults to, 110–111
   trust in one's, 78–79, 82, 83
   vajrayana, 56
Irritation, 84
   bliss and, 129
   intellect and, 80–81
   mahamudra experience and, 119–120, 129

Jnana ("wisdom"), 68, 72, 95, 148
   kingdom principle and, 83

Kagyu lineage teachings, 16, 19
Karma
   American, 51
   gap and, 47–48
   meditation practice and, 48
   miracles and, 139
   national, 26, 139–140
Kingdom principle, 83
Knowledge, 72
   See also Prajna
Kundalini yoga, 142

Lavapa (mahasiddha), 138
Life
   Disneyland quality of, 137–138
   as mirage, 50, 137–138, 147–149

The Life and Teachings of Naropa
   (Guenther), 4–6
Logic, 6, 22
   insanity and, 16
Luminosity (Tib. *ösel*), 51, 138

Madness, 16, 22–23
   ego and, 23
Magic, 100–101
   simplicity and, 133
Mahamudra ("great symbol"), 3, 15–16, 93, 108, 116–130
   basic sanity and, 131
   clarity as, 116, 131, 134
   confidence and, 131
   as "crazy wisdom," 120
   definition of, 116
   irritation and, 119–120, 129
   levels of, 131–150
   nonduality and, 118
   "ordinary consciousness" and, 118–119, 146
   samsara/nirvana and, 125
   wisdom of, 118
Mahamudra experience, 19, 50
   coemergent wisdom as, 118
   hallucinogenic experience vs., 127
   ordinariness as camouflage of, 118–119
   pain and, 127–128
   shunyata vs., 117–118
   vividness of, 117
   youthful quality of, 118
Mahayana ("big vehicle"), 30, 55
   grandioseness, 145
   sacredness, 144–145
   teacher, 122
Mandala, 132
Manjushri, sword of, 78–79
Mantra, 56–57
Meditation in action, 144
Meditation practice, 28, 48–49, 141
   karma and, 48

as primordial gesture, 49
shunyata and, 99, 117
technique, 33
Message(s), 148
tantric, 120, 122–123
"tomorrow," 107–108, 111
Mind, 42–44, 56–57
analytical vs. intellectual, 75–77
body and, 56
inquisitive (Tib. *gyuwa*), 42–43
as mirror, 44
protection (mantra), 57
Mindfulness practice, 126
awareness and, 143–144
as recollection (Skt. *smriti*), 143
shunyata and, 90
Miracle(s), 139–140, 142
karma and, 139
Mirage
memory as, 149
as rainbow realm, 122, 125
reality as, 50, 137–138, 147–148
Monastic life, 71
See also Naropa, monastic life
Moral law, 23–24, 110

Naiveté, 91–92
as obstacle to well-being, 133–134
Nakedness, 121–122, 129
Nalanda University, 71, 103, 109
Naropa (Tib. *'Jig-med grags-pa*),
151n.1–1
as everyman, 113–114
Marpa and, 149–150
monastic life, 58, 67–68, 71, 75,
88
Nalanda University and, 71, 103,
109
old woman (Vajrayogini) and, 5–6,
88–89, 94–95, 114–115
six doctrines of, 50–51, 136–139,
152n.6–1
suicide attempt, 41–42, 121

Tilopa and, 3, 14, 18, 32–35, 41,
50, 68, 101, 104–105, 121
twelve trials of, 7–20, 22, 37–38,
45–46, 101–115, 124, 130
Nirmanakaya, 55
Nonduality, 75
mahamudra and, 118
pain of, 126
shunyata and, 91, 117–118

Old woman/Vajrayogini, 5–6, 22, 88–
89, 94–95, 114–115
Ordinariness, 95
well-being and, 146
Ordinary mind/consciousness, 118–
119, 146

Pain, 55–71, 96–97, 126–128
aggression and, 70
ego and, 57
energy and, 63
fascination with, 64
hope and, 55–68
intellect and, 71
mahamudra and, 126, 127–128
pleasure and, 29, 68, 97
prajna and, 74–75
shunyata and, 97
as start of continuity, 96
vajrayana, 56–57, 113
Paranoia, 19, 31
Passion, 84
Perception, 148
Phowa ("ejection of consciousness"),
138
death and, 140
Pleasure
as bliss, 121
mahamudra and, 120–121
spiritual materialism and, 120
Pop art, 17–18
Prajna ("supreme knowledge"), 72–85,
95

analogy: licking frosty rock in win-
     ter, 73–74
awareness and, 72
compassion and, 82
emotions and, 76–78, 79–81
energy and, 82
irritation and, 80–81, 82
jnana (wisdom) and, 68, 72, 82–83
as mother of all buddhas, 89
pain and, 74–75
resentment and, 72, 80
shunyata and, 87–90, 92
skillful means and, 79
as sword of Manjushri, 78–79, 80
tantra and, 82
trust in oneself and, 83
Projection(s), 20–21, 36, 39–40
process of, 44–45
vajra pride and, 121
Psychosomatic tension, 136–137

Rainbow realm, 122, 125
Reality (ultimate truth), 33–34, 37,
     73–74
accident and, 34
body and, 33, 47
dream/mirage as, 147–149
pain of, 113
prajna and, 74
as shadow of dreams, 46, 47
Reassurance, need for
as one-eyed effigy, 30–31
paranoia and, 19, 31
Reference point(s), 64
awareness as, 93
vajrayana, 145–146
wisdom as vajra, 146
Resentment
emotions and, 84–86
intelligence and, 84
prajna and, 72, 79–80, 84–85
Retreat, 18
Rudrahood, 98

Sacredness, 132–134
mahayana, 144–145
obviousness and, 133
theistic, 132, 144–145
vajrayana, 132–133
well-being and, 133
Samaya discipline, 107, 128
Sambhogakaya, 55
Samsara, 23, 89
characteristics of, 115
conceptual mind and, 49
nonexistence of, 125
as stepping stones to enlightenment,
     44
Sanity/insanity, 16–17, 22, 28
Satori, 94
Seeing/looking
fearlessness and, 78
vs. look-and-see, 83
prajna/jnana as, 72
Self-consciousness, 27, 86
Sense perceptions, 135
Shunyata, 87–98, 116, 152n.4–1
aggression and, 95
aloneness and, 93
beyond, 100–115
compassion and, 89, 96
as consort of all buddhas, 89
ego and, 99, 126
emptiness/fullness of, 130
as feminine principle, 89
habitual thoughts and, 109
hinayana experience of, 98
impermanence as glimpse of, 98
mahamudra vs., 117–118
nonduality and, 91, 117–118, 126
pain and, 97, 112–113
prajna and, 87–90, 92
samsara/nirvana and, 125
satori as, 94
twelve trials and, 88, 130
Vajrayogini as, 88

vipashyana and, 99
visualization and, 140–141
Six doctrines of Naropa, 50–51,
    136–139
  in order of explication:
  inner heat *(tumo),* 136–137
  illusory body *(gyulü),* 137
  dream *(milam),* 137–138
  luminosity *(ösel),* 138
  transference *(phowa),* 138, 140
  sleep (bardo state), 138–139,
    152n.6–1
Skillful means (Skt. *upaya),* 131
Sleep
  as bardo/in-between state, 138–140,
    152n.6–1
Soft spot/nonaggression, 83–84, 89
Space, 64–65, 130
  as great umbrella above little um-
    brellas, 65
Spiritual friend, 34, 35–37, 40, 65
Spiritual materialism, 28, 61, 92
Spiritual operation, 32–49
Spiritual path, 62
Spiritual practice, 4
  ego and, 28–29
Student/teacher relationship.
  See Teacher/student relationship
Sudden glimpse
  illusory body and, 50
  satori as, 94
Suffering
  cause of, 36
  truth of (Skt. *duhkha satya),* 60
  See also Pain
Sword of Manjushri, 78–79
Symbolism, 37–38
  of ego, 42
  fascination with, 26
  mahamudra, 3, 15–16, 116

Taking refuge, 60
Tantra, 55, 94–96
  as continuity, 64

energy and, 82
killing parents metaphor, 107
prajna and, 82
sense perceptions and, 135, 136
See also Mahamudra; Vajrayana
Teacher/student relationship, 4, 32–
    38, 40–41, 94–95
  hinayana, 122
  mahayana, 122
  vajrayana, 122–123, 125, 128–130
  See also Guru; Vajra master
Teachings, identification with, 93, 97
Theism, 132, 141
Three-yana principle, 123–124
Tilopa, 3, 14, 18, 41, 50, 68, 101,
    121
  and moral law, 23–24
  discovery of, 32–35, 102–103
  Vajrayogini and, 115
"Tomorrow" messages, 107–108, 111
Transcendental vandalism, 91
Transference of consciousness (Tib.
    phowa), 51
Trickery, 100–101, 110
  enlightenment and, 145
Trust in oneself, 78–79, 81–82, 83
Truth, 19, 33
  pain and, 70
  sacredness and, 133
  of suffering (Skt. *duhkha satya),* 60
Tumo ("inner heat"), 136–137
Twelve trials of Naropa, 7–20, 22, 45–
    46, 101–115, 124
  aggression and, 102–104
  ignorance and, 102, 106–109
  passion and, 102, 104–106
  shunyata and, 130
  symbolism of, 37–38
  as unlearning process, 38
Two veils (conflicting emotions/wrong
    beliefs), 38

Vajra ("adamantine"), 134
Vajra master, 131

Vajra pride, 121
Vajrayana ("diamond vehicle"), 55–56,
    124, 127–134, 140–141, 145–
    146
  bodhisattva action and, 127
  relationship with elements, 140
  sacredness, 132–133
  sadhana practice, 134
  teacher: like a pill/seed in you,
    128–130
  teacher-student, 122–123, 125,
    128–130
  See also Mahamudra; Tantra
Vajrayogini
  as old woman, 5–6, 88–89, 94–95,
    114–115
  as symbol of shunyata, 88
  Tilopa and, 115
Visualization, 134–135
  shunyata and, 140–141

Wakefulness vs. awareness, 139
Watcher, 27, 29
Watts, Alan, 27
Well-being
  hopelessness and, 67
  obstacle to, 133–134
  sacredness and, 133–134
Western practitioners, 141–142
  theism and, 141
Wisdom (Skt. *jnana*), 68, 95
  kingdom principle and, 83
  vs. knowledge, 72
  as vajra reference point, 146
Words/sense, 5–6, 22
  prajna/jnana and, 95
Wrong beliefs about reality, 38

Yidam, 134–135

Zen Buddhism, 94, 152n.4–1

ALSO IN THE DHARMA OCEAN SERIES

Crazy Wisdom
The Heart of the Buddha
Journey without Goal: The Tantric Wisdom of the Buddha
The Lion's Roar: An Introduction to Tantra
Orderly Chaos: The Mandala Principle
Transcending Madness: The Experience of the Six Bardos